D0379914

BORROWING DESIGNS FROM OTHER CRAFTS

Another Amish quilt pattern, the Bars design, *above,* inspired the handsome knitted throw, *right.* An unusual mix of three striking colors and four textured stitches (see close-ups, *above right*) yields a design that's dramatically different, yet at home in almost any setting.

Other patchwork patterns that translate well into knit and crochet designs include Log Cabin patterns, variations of four- and nine-patch blocks, Trip-Around-the-World or Sunshine-and-Shadow motifs, and other designs constructed from simple geometric shapes such as right-angle triangles, squares, and rectangles.

See page 202 for instructions for this 45x56-inch throw.

Borrowing Designs From Other Crafts

Cross-stitch designs are made to order for filet crochet enthusiasts. To prove the point, we've translated the floral motif on the pillowcase, *below,* into the beautiful, airy pattern on the lacy curtains at *left.*

When selecting a cross-stitch design to crochet, look for a pattern that relies on shape and spacing, rather than color changes, to define individual elements in the design. Test the design's suitability for filet crochet by charting the pattern on graph paper, using a single color to mark all the squares for each filled-in portion of the motif. If each of the elements in the design remains legible, then the pattern should work well in filet crochet.

Instructions for the curtain begin on page 204.

Petite Treasures

Delicate Crocheted Keepsakes

Intricate patterns worked in colorful cotton threads yield the small yet exquisite delights showcased on these pages. Here you'll find the perfect memento for any sentimental occasion—including doily-pattern pillows, fanciful nosegays, sweet sachets, and a dainty assortment of boxes and baskets to crochet for milady's chamber.

Doilies worked in pastel shades of pearl cotton are paired with shimmery chintz fabrics for the flirty little boudoir pillows pictured here. Used singly or piled in extravagant profusion, doily pillows have a deliciously feminizing effect on any style love seat or sofa, or in any bedroom. Directions for all projects shown in this chapter begin on page 118.

DELICATE CROCHETED KEEPSAKES

Irish crochet is easily identified by its three-dimensional rosettes and other flowers and leaves set into an intricate network of lace. The square insert on the napkin, *above,* and the clover-leaf edging on the doily atop the piano, *opposite,* are elegant examples of Irish crochet in its most traditional form.

For the bouquets, we've treated six typical Irish crochet motifs in a most *untraditional* manner. Lightly starched and supported with wire, the designs become fanciful, free-standing blossoms and leaves. Mix these crocheted flowers (roses, pansies, shamrocks, clover, and leaves) with delicate baby's breath for a lovely arrangement like the one *above.*

Tucked into the nosegay, *opposite,* are simpler versions of the same blossoms. Sparked with pearl stamens and combined with real or silk flowers, they comprise a bouquet that any bride would be proud to carry—and any bridesmaid delighted to catch.

DELICATE CROCHETED KEEPSAKES

Sensational presents *do* come in small packages, and in this case the package itself is an extraordinary treasure. Measuring less than 6 inches in diameter, the crocheted basket of blossoms adorning the top of the trinket box pictured here has all the vibrant color and exquisite detail of a hand-painted Persian miniature.

The lacy basket is worked in conventional white crochet cotton. But the dozens of different blossoms are crocheted in every color of the rainbow from an eclectic assortment of threads, including buttonhole twist, regular sewing thread, embroidery floss, and pearl cotton.

Like the larger flowers on the preceding pages, these miniature blossoms are three-dimensional. Each tiny petal is carefully stretched and shaped with a stiffening mixture of white glue and water, and the finished arrangement is accented with tiny beads, seed pearls, and a scattering of dewlike rhinestones for extra sparkle.

To make the box shown, tack the flower-laden basket to a circle of black taffeta, and fit it into the recessed lid of a purchased wooden box.

Or, adapt the same design to complement a different-shape box or frame. Refer to the close-up photograph, *above,* for inspiration, or create your own arrangement and color scheme.

DELICATE CROCHETED KEEPSAKES

Whether a cache for diamonds and pearls or just a lot of dime-store glitter, the lacy jewel box, *above,* makes a lovely addition to a dressing table or chest of drawers.

The 3x3x6-inch box is assembled from cardboard, padded with fleece, and covered with chintz fabric. Then block the crocheted cover and tack into place.

You'll find more sweet little somethings in the pretty pastels, *opposite*. A quick-to-crochet collection of diminutive sachets adds a pleasing scent to your own or a friend's drawers or closets.

Or stitch a pair of dainty baskets to hold your favorite tiny treasures, a small bouquet of flowers, or the Easter Bunny's offering. Soak the baskets in a glue and water solution, then slip them over a conveniently shaped glass or jar until the solution hardens and the shape becomes permanent.

Spread beneath the sachets and baskets is a doily of unusual design and pleasing proportions. Half-circles of crocheted lace fan out from each side of a linen hankie, making it a perfect centerpiece for tabletop or dresser.

Crocheted Square Pillow

Shown on page 110.
Pillow is 10 inches square, excluding ruffle.

MATERIALS

DMC Pearl Cotton, Size 3 (50-gram ball): 1 ball No. 352 orange
Size E aluminum crochet hook
1 yard of chintz to make pillow form; scraps of contrasting chintz to cover cording
2½ yards of narrow cotton cording
Polyester fiberfill

Abbreviations: Page 211.
Gauge: 1 motif = 3-inch square.

INSTRUCTIONS

Ch 8, join with sl st to form ring.

FIRST MOTIF *Rnd 1:* Ch 1, work 16 sc in ring, join with sl st to first sc.

Rnd 2: Ch 8, dc in same st used for joining, * ch 3, sk sc, sc in next sc, ch 3, sk sc; in next sc work dc, ch 5, dc. Rep from * around; end ch 3, sk sc, sc in next sc, ch 3, join with sl st to third ch of ch-8 at beg of rnd.

Rnd 3: Ch 3, * in next ch-lp make **4 dc, ch 5, 4 dc—corner made;** dc in next dc, ch 3, sk next 2 ch-3 lps, dc in next dc; rep from * around; end ch 3, sk 2 ch-3 lps, join with sl st to top of ch-3.

Rnd 4: Ch 3, dc in next 4 dc, * in ch-5 corner lp work 4 dc, ch 2, 4 dc; dc in next 5 dc; ch 2, sc in next ch-3 lp, ch 2, dc in next 5 dc; rep from * around; end ch 2, join with sl st to top of ch-3; fasten off.

SECOND MOTIF: Work as for First Motif through Rnd 3.

Rnd 4: Ch 3, dc in next 4 dc, * in corner lp work 4 dc, ch 1, drop hook from work and insert hook in any corner ch-2 lp on First Motif, draw dropped lp through, ch 1, 4 dc in same corner lp of second motif. Dc in next 5 dc, drop hook from work, insert hook in corresponding dc on First Motif, draw dropped lp through, ch 2, sc in ch-2 lp on Second Motif, ch 2, drop hook from work, insert hook in next dc on First Motif, draw dropped lp through, dc in next 5 dc on Second Motif. In corner lp work 4 dc, ch 1, drop hook from work, insert hook in corresponding ch-2 corner lp of First Motif, draw dropped lp through, ch 1, work 4 dc in same corner lp on Second Motif. Complete rnd as for Rnd 4 of First Motif; fasten off.

THIRD MOTIF: Work as for Second Motif.

FOURTH MOTIF: Work as for Second Motif, except join motif to First Motif to begin a new row.

Rem 5 motifs will have 2 side joinings. Work joinings as for Second Motif, except at corners where three motifs join tog. Work these corners as follows: In corner lp work 4 dc, ch 1, drop hook from work, insert hook in corresponding corner lp, draw dropped lp through, drop hook from work, sk next corner, insert hook in corner lp of next corner motif, draw dropped lp through, ch 1, 4 dc in same corner lp of motif in progress. Complete rem joinings as established for Second Motif. Block piece.

ASSEMBLY (For the ruffled pillows): Cut 2 pieces of chintz 1 inch larger than the blocked piece for front and back; set aside. Cut 8-inch strips of chintz for ruffling to measure twice the perimeter; sew strips together to make tube. Fold strip in half, wrong sides together and run gathering threads along raw edges; then gather to fit front pillow edge. Cover cording with contrasting fabric and baste to pillow top. With right sides together, sew ruffle atop cording, then sew pillow back to pillow front, leaving an opening for turning. Clip seams, turn, stuff, and sew opening closed.

(For the boxed pillow): Cut chintz for pillow front and back as for ruffled pillow. Cut 2½-inch-wide boxing strip to fit outside dimensions of pillow; set aside. Cover 2 pieces of cotton cording with contrasting fabric to fit outside dimensions of pillow. Baste, then sew cording to front and back of pillow. With right sides together, sew boxing strip to pillow front and back, leaving an opening for turning. Clip seams, turn, stuff, sew opening closed.

Crocheted Round Pillow

Shown on pages 110–111.
Pillow is 12 inches in diameter, excluding ruffles.

MATERIALS

DMC Pearl Cotton, Size 3 (50-gram ball): 1 ball No. 807 blue
Size 3 steel crochet hook
1 yard chintz for pillow form and ruffling; scraps of contrasting chintz to cover cording
1 yard narrow cotton cording
Polyester fiberfill

Abbreviations: Page 211.

INSTRUCTIONS

Ch 8, join with sl st to form ring.

Rnd 1: Ch 1, work 20 sc in ring; join with sl st to first sc.

Rnd 2: Ch 3, dc in next sc, * ch 1, dc in each of next 2 sc; rep from * around; end ch 1, join with sl st to top of ch-3 at beg of rnd.

Rnd 3: Ch 3, dc in next dc; * 2 dc in ch-1 sp, dc in each of next 2 dc; rep from * around; end 2 dc in ch-1 sp, sl st to top of ch-3 at beg of rnd—40 dc.

Rnd 4: Ch 1, sc in same st as join, ch 5, * sk 3 dc, sl st in next dc, ch 5; rep from * around; end sl st to first sc at beg of rnd.

Rnd 5: In *each* ch-5 lp around work (sc, hdc, 3 dc, trc, ch 1, trc, 3 dc, hdc, sc). Join with sl st to first sc at beg of rnd.

Rnd 6: Sl st in next 5 sts, sc in ch-1 sp, * ch 8, sc in next ch-1 sp; rep from * around; join with sl st to first sc at beg of rnd.

Rnd 7: Work 12 sc in *each* ch-8 lp around; join with sl st to first sc—120 sc.

Rnd 8: Ch 5, * sk 2 sc, dc in next sc, ch 2; rep from * around; join last ch-2 to third ch of ch-5 at beg of rnd—40 ch-2 lps.

Rnd 9: Ch 3, * 4 dc in next ch-2 lp, dc in next dc; rep from * around; end 4 dc in last ch-2 lp, join to top of ch-3 at beg of rnd—200 dc.

Rnd 10: Ch 5, * sk 3 dc, dc in next dc, ch 2; rep from * around; join last ch-2 to third ch of ch-5 at beg of rnd—50 ch-2 lps.

Rnd 11: Sl st into next ch-2 lp, ch 3, in same lp make 2 dc, ch 3, 3 dc; * sk next ch-2 lp; in following ch-2 lp work 3 dc, ch 3, 3 dc; rep from * around; end sk last ch-2 lp, join to top of ch-3 at beg of rnd.

Rnd 12: Sl st in next 2 dc and into ch-3 sp, ch 3, in same ch-3 sp work 8 dc; * in next ch-3 sp work 9 dc—shell made; rep from * around, join to top of ch-3 at beg of rnd—25 shell grps.

Rnd 13: Sl st in next 5 dc, ch 1, sc in same st as last sl st, * ch 8, sl st in center dc of next shell grp; rep from * around; end ch 8, join to first sc.

Rnd 14: In *each* ch-8 lp around work 12 sc, join to first sc; fasten off.

Assemble pillow using instructions for Square Pillow, page 118.

Crocheted Snowflake Pillow

Shown on page 110.
Pillow is 12 inches in diameter, excluding ruffles.

Abbreviations: Page 211.

MATERIALS

DMC Pearl Cotton, Size 3 (50-gram ball): 1 ball No. 993 green
Size 3 steel crochet hook
1 yard chintz for pillow form and ruffle; scraps of contrasting chintz to cover cording
1 yard narrow cotton cording
Polyester fiberfill

INSTRUCTIONS

Ch 5, join with sl st to form ring.

Rnd 1: Ch 3, work 19 dc in ring; join with sl st to top of ch-3 at beg of rnd.

Rnd 2: (Ch 5, sk dc, sc in next dc) 9 times; ch 5, join with sl st to sl st at end of Rnd 1.

Rnd 3: Sl st in each of next 3 ch of ch-5 lp, ch 1, sc in same lp, (ch 5, sc in next ch-5 lp) 9 times; ch 5, join with sl st in sc at beg of rnd.

Rnd 4: Sl st in each of next 3 ch, ch 1, sc in same lp, (ch 6, sc in next ch-5 lp) 9 times; ch 6, join with sl st in sc at beg of rnd.

Rnd 5: Sl st into ch-6 lp, ch 3, in same lp work 3 dc, ch 2, 4 dc; (in next ch-6 lp work 4 dc, ch 2, 4 dc) 9 times; join with sl st in top of ch-3.

Rnd 6: Sl st in next 2 dc, ch 3, dc in next dc, * in ch-2 sp work 2 dc, ch 2, 2 dc; dc in next 2 dc; ch 2, sk 4 dc, dc in next 2 dc; rep from * around; join last ch-2 in top of ch-3 at beg of rnd.

Rnd 7: Sl st in next 2 dc, ch 3, dc in next dc; * in ch-2 sp work 2 dc, ch 2, 2 dc; dc in next 2 dc, ch 3, sc in next ch-2 lp, ch 3, sk 2 dc, dc in next 2 dc; rep from * around; join last ch-3 in top of ch-3 at beg of rnd.

Rnd 8: Sl st in next 2 dc, ch 3, dc in next dc; * in ch-2 sp work 2 dc, ch 2, 2 dc, dc in next 2 dc; (ch 3, sc in next ch-3 lp) twice, ch 3, sk 2 dc, dc in next 2 dc; rep from * around; join last ch-3 to top of ch-3 at beg of rnd.

Rnd 9: Rep Rnd 8 except rep between ( )s 3 times.

Rnd 10: Sl st in next 3 dc and ch-2 sp; ch 3, in same sp work 2 dc, ch 1, 3 dc; * (ch 1, in next ch-3 sp work 3 dc) 4 times; ch 1, sk 4 dc, in next ch-2 sp work 3 dc, ch 1, 3 dc; rep from * around; join last ch-1 to top of ch-3 at beg of rnd.

Rnd 11: Sl st in next 2 dc and ch-1 sp; ch 1, in same sp work sc, hdc, dc, hdc, sc; * sc in center dc of 3-dc grp; in next ch-1 sp work sc, hdc, dc, hdc, sc, rep from * around, join to first sc at beg of rnd; fasten off.

Assemble pillow using instructions for Square Pillow, page 118.

Crocheted Flowers And Leaves

Shown on page 112.

MATERIALS

Coats and Clark Knit-Cro-Sheen: 1 ball *each* of several pastel colors
Size 6 steel crochet hook
Florist's tape and wire
Spray starch

Abbreviations: Page 211.

INSTRUCTIONS

Work the 6 flower and leaf motifs that follow in the amounts and colors desired. Block each piece and saturate with spray starch. Insert 1 end of a wire length into the "stem" end of the flower or leaf, and wrap lower end of flower and entire length of wire with florist's tape.

continued

PANSY: Ch 7, join with sl st to form ring.

Rnd 1: Ch 1, work 18 sc in ring; join with sl st to first sc.

Rnd 2: Ch 1, sc in same st as joining, (ch 7, sk next 5 sc, sc in next sc) twice; ch 7, join with sl st to first sc.

Rnd 3: Ch 1, in *each* ch-7 lp around work 17 sc; join with sl st to first sc.

PANSY PETALS: ** *Row 1:* (Ch 4, sk next sc, sc in next sc) 8 times; ch 4; turn—8 ch-4 lps.

Row 2: (Sc in next ch-4 lp, ch 4) 7 times; sc in last ch-4 lp, ch 1; turn.

Row 3: Over *each* ch-4 lp work 4 sc, sl st into last sc of Row 1, ch 1; turn.

Row 4: (Sc in next 8 sc, **ch 5, sl st in fifth ch from hook—picot made**) 3 times; sc in last 8 sc, sl st in turning ch at end of Row 2; fasten off—1 petal made.

** With right side facing, join thread in first sc of next 17-sc grp and rep between **s 2 times more.

ROSE: Ch 7, join with sl st to form ring.

Rnd 1: Ch 1, work 18 sc in ring; join with sl st to first sc.

Rnd 2: Ch 5, sk 2 sc, sc in next sc, (ch 3, sk 2 sc, sc in next sc) 4 times; ch 3, sl st in second ch of ch-5 at beg of rnd—6 ch-3 lps.

Rnd 3: Over *each* ch-3 lp work sc, 4 dc, and sc; sl st to first sc.

Rnd 4: (Ch 4, holding petals forward, work dc around the post from the back of next sc on Rnd 2) 6 times; do not join.

Rnd 5: Over *each* ch-4 lp around work sc, 7 dc, and sc; join with sl st to first sc.

Rnd 6: (Ch 5, holding petals forward, work dc around post from the back of next dc on Rnd 4) 6 times; do not join.

Rnd 7: Over *each* ch-5 lp work sc, 10 dc, and sc; join with sl st to first sc.

Rnd 8: (Ch 6, work dc around post from the back of next dc on Rnd 6) 6 times; do not join.

Rnd 9: Over *each* ch-6 lp work sc, 13 dc, and sc; join with sl st to first sc; fasten off.

PALM LEAF: Ch 12, join with sl st to form ring.

Rnd 1: Ch 1, work 30 sc in ring; join with sl st to first sc.

Row 1: Ch 1, sc in each of next 12 sc; ch 4, turn.

Row 2: Sk first sc, sc in next sc; (ch 4, sk sc, sc in next sc) 5 times—6 ch-4 lps; ch 4, turn.

Row 3: Sc in first ch-4 lp, (ch 4, sc in next ch-4 lp) 4 times—5 ch-4 lps; ch 1, turn.

Row 4: Over *each* ch-4 lp work 4 sc—20 sc; ch 8, turn.

Row 5: Sk first 6 sc, sc in next sc, ch 8, sk next 5 sc, sc in next sc, ch 8, sk 6 sc, sc in last sc—3 ch-8 lps; ch 1, turn.

Row 6: Over *each* ch-8 lp work 14 sc; sl st in the side of work next row down; continue along side of work with 4 more sl sts to Rnd 1; sc in each of next 8 sc on ch-12 ring.

Ch 10 for stem, sk first ch, sc in next 9 ch; sc in each rem sc on ch-12 ring to beg of leaf; sl st up side of leaf; end with sl st in first sc of Row 4; fasten off.

SHAMROCK: Ch 8, join with sl st to form ring.

Rnd 1: Ch 1, work 12 sc in ring; join with sl st to first sc.

Rnd 2: (Ch 8, sk next 4 sc, sl st in next sc) twice; ch 8; *do not turn.*

Rnd 3: Over *each* ch-8 lp work sc, 13 dc and sc; join with sl st in beg ch-8 lp of Rnd 2.

Ch 14 for stem; sc in second ch from hook and next 11 ch, sl st in last ch; fasten off.

CLOVER LEAF: Ch 12, sl st in first ch to form ring.

Rnd 1: Ch 1, work 22 sc in ring; join with sl st to first sc.

Rnd 2: * Ch 10, sl st in next sc on ch-12 ring, rotate work, (do not turn) and work 17 sc in ch-10 ring just made.

Continuing around ch-10 ring, sc in next 3 sc, dc in next 11 sc, sc in next 3 sc; working on ch-12 ring, sc in next 2 sc; rep from * twice more; end last rep with sc in next 8 sc on ch-12 ring.

Ch 10 for stem, sc in second ch from hook and next 8 ch, sc in rem sc on ch-12 ring; sl st in sp below first leaf; fasten off.

LEAF: * Ch 16. *Row 1:* Sc in second ch from hook and next 14 ch; ch 1, turn.

Row 2: Sc in first 3 sc, dc in next 2 sc, (ch 2, sk next sc, dc in next sc) 3 times; ch 2, sk next sc, sc in next sc, sl st in next sc; ch 1, turn.

Row 3: Sk first st, sl st in next sc, (2 sc in next ch-2 sp, sc in next dc) 3 times, 2 sc in next ch-2 sp, sc in next 4 sts, sl st in last st—1 petal of leaf completed; do not fasten off. Rep from * twice more.

Stack petals with last one on top and work a sl st through all 3 petals ⅛ inch in from lower tip to secure.

Ch 14 for stem, sc in second ch from hook and each rem ch. Sl st again through all petals; fasten off.

Refer to the directions at the beginning of the instructions for finishing and assembly.

Crocheted Nosegay

Shown on page 113.

MATERIALS
DMC Pearl Cotton, Size 8 (95-yard balls): 1 ball *each* of No. 353 peach, No. 725 dark yellow, No. 727 light yellow, No. 3326 pink, No. 602 magenta, No. 552 purple, No. 809 blue, No. 827 light blue, No. 955 light green, No. 912 green, No. 993 apple green
Size 8 steel crochet hook
Florist's tape and wire
Purchased pearl stamens
Purchased silk flowers
Baby's breath
Nosegay holder

Abbreviations: Page 211.

INSTRUCTIONS
Assemble flowers as for crocheted flowers, see page 119. Separate pearl stamens and arrange in flower petals as desired, securing in place with florist tape. Arrange flowers into nosegay with purchased silk flowers and baby's breath and place in nosegay holder.

PANSY: Work as for first 3 rnds of pansy pat, page 120.

Next rnd: * (Ch 4, sk next sc, sc in next sc) 8 times; sl st in sc bet ch-7 lp; rep from * around; join with sl st to first ch of ch-4 at beg of rnd; fasten off.

ROSE: Work as for rose pat, page 120, through Rnd 5; fasten off.

PALM LEAF: Ch 9, join with sl st to form ring.

Rnd 1: Ch 1, work 24 sc in ring, join with sl st to first sc.

Rows 1–3: Work as for Rows 1–3 of palm leaf pat page 120.

Row 4: Work as for Row 4; ch 7, turn.

Row 5: Work as for Row 5, except ch 7, in lieu of ch 8.

Row 6: Over each ch-7 lp work 12 sc; sl st in side of work next row down; continue along side of work with 4 more sl sts to Rnd 1; sc in each of next 7 sc on ch-12 ring.

Ch 10 for stem; sk first ch, sc in next 9 ch; sc in each rem sc on ch-12 ring to beg of leaf; sl st up side of leaf; end with sl st in first sc of Row 4; fasten off.

SHAMROCK: Work as for shamrock pat, page 120.

CLOVER LEAF: Ch 8, join with sl st to form ring.

Rnd 1: Ch 1, work 16 sc in ring; join with sl st to first sc.

Rnd 2: * Ch 8, sl st in next sc; do not turn; rotate work and make 14 sc in ch-8 ring just made; continue working around ch-8 ring making sc in next 2 sc, hdc in next sc, dc in next 8 sc, hdc in next sc, sc in next 2 sc; sc in next 2 sc on ch-8 ring; rep from * 2 times more; end sc in next 6 sc on ch-8 ring, ch 10 for stem, sc in second ch from hook and in next 8 ch; sc in rem sc on ch-8 ring, sl st in sp below first leaf; fasten off.

Crocheted Rose Motif and Napkin

Shown on page 112.
Finished size of napkin is 14 inches square.

MATERIALS
15x15-inch square of white lightweight linen or purchased napkin
Clark's Big Ball 3-Cord Crochet Cotton, Size 30: 1 ball white
Size 12 steel crochet hook

Abbreviations: See page 211.

INSTRUCTIONS
ROSETTE: Beg at center, ch 5, join with sl st to form ring.

Rnd 1: Ch 6, * dc in ring, ch 3; rep from * 6 times more; join with sl st to third ch of beg ch-6—8 ch-3 lps.

Rnd 2: Over *each* ch-3 lp work sc, hdc, 3 dc, hdc, sc—8 petals.

Rnd 3: * Ch 5, holding petals of rose forward, work sc around post of next dc in Rnd 1; rep from * 7 times more—8 ch-5 lps.

Rnd 4: Over *each* ch-5 lp work sc, hdc, 5 dc, hdc, sc—8 petals.

Rnd 5: * Ch 7, holding petals of rose forward, work sc around post of next sc in Rnd 3; rep from * 7 times more—8 ch-7 lps.

Rnd 6: Over *each* ch-7 lp work sc, hdc, 7 dc, hdc, sc—8 petals.

Rnd 7: * Ch 9, work sc around post of next sc in Rnd 5; rep from * 7 times more—8 ch-9 lps.

Rnd 8: Over *each* ch-9 lp work sc, hdc, 9 dc, hdc, sc; join with sl st to first sc—rosette made; do not fasten off.

LAYING THE ROSETTE IN THE BACKGROUND: *Rnd 1:* Sl st in each of first 3 sts of petal, ch 1, sc in same st as last sl st, [** ch 13, **sl st in seventh ch from hook—picot made; (ch 7, sl st in seventh ch from hook) twice; sl st in same ch as for making first picot—picot grp made;** **. Ch 6, sc in tenth st of same petal. Rep bet **s once; ch 6, sc in seventh st of next petal; rep bet **s once, ch 6, sc in fourth st of next petal]. Rep bet the [ ]s 3 times more; end ch 6, sl st in sc at beg of rnd—12 picot grps made.

Rnd 2: Sl st in each ch to first picot grp, sc in back of work around the 2 upright bars of center picot; ** ch 13, work picot grp, ch 6, sc in back of work around the 2 upright bars of center picot of next picot grp, ch 11, sc in back of next picot grp; ch 2; *turn;* work 12 sc over ch-11 lp, ch 1; *turn;* sc in each sc, ch 1, *turn;* ch 6, sk 2 sc, sc in next sc, (ch 6, sk 3 sc, sc in next sc) twice; *turn;* over each ch-6 lp work sc, hdc, 6 dc, hdc, and sc; work 4 sl sts along side of work to next picot grp; sc in same st as ch-11 join; ch 13, work picot grp, ch 6, sc in back of center picot of next picot grp **. Rep bet **s 3 times more; end ch 6, sl st in first sc at beg of rnd.

continued

Rnd 3: Sl st in each ch to first picot grp, sc in back of center picot of next picot grp; ch 13, work picot grp, ch 6, ** sc in the fifth st of first scallop; ch 13, work picot grp, ch 6, sc in first st of second scallop; ch 13, work picot grp, ch 6, sc in tenth st of second scallop; ch 13, work picot grp, ch 6, sc in sixth st of third scallop; (ch 13, work picot grp, ch 6, sc in back of center picot of next picot grp) twice; ch 13, work picot grp, ch 6 **. Rep bet **s 3 times more working in succeeding scallops around; end ch 6, sl st into sc at beg of rnd; fasten off.

FINISHING: Block motif. Trim fabric square and hem to make 14-inch square. Position motif in 1 corner; baste in place. Using sharp scissors, cut away fabric behind motif, leaving ¼-inch seam allowance. Turn back ¼-inch seam allowance and hemstitch in place, tacking the motif to secure as you work.

Crocheted Clover Leaf Doily Edging

Shown on page 113.
Doily is 10 inches in diameter.

MATERIALS

DMC Cébélia Crochet Cotton, Size 20: 1 ball white
Size 8 steel crochet hook
9-inch square of linen or cotton fabric

Abbreviations: Page 211.

INSTRUCTIONS

For fabric center

Pre-wash fabric to shrink. With pencil, draw circle on fabric around 8-inch-diameter plate. Machine-stitch around pencil line, then make another row of stitching just outside first line. Press fabric to back inside first row of stitching, then trim outside of second row. Work 250 sc evenly spaced around fabric circle through both layers, join with sl st in first sc.

NOTE: This edging may be made on any size round or oval fabric center, using coarser or finer thread if desired. Prepare fabric as above and crochet closely around edge, having total number of sc a multiple of 10.

EDGING: *Row 1:* Sc in same sc as sl st; * **(ch 5, sl st in third ch from hook—picot made) twice,** ch 8, sc in fifth ch from hook (base of clover); ch 4, *turn.* (Sc in the ch-5 lp formed by the sc in fifth ch from hook, ch 4) twice, sc in base of clover lp, *turn;* (in next ch-4 lp work hdc, 6 dc, hdc, sl st in next sc) 3 times; ch 5, sl st in third st from hook, sl st in base of corresponding picot, ch 5, sl st in third st from hook, ch 2, sk next 4 sc on circle, sc in fifth sc; rep from * around; end sl st in first sc at beg of rnd; fasten off.

Row 2: Ch 5, sl st in third from hook, ch 3, fasten thread with sl st in center top leaf of any clover. * (Ch 6, sl st in third ch from hook) 3 times, ch 3, sl st in center of third leaf on same clover, ch 3, trc in space between picots of next big lp on first row, ch 3, sl st in center of first leaf on next clover, ch 3, sl st in last picot made, (ch 6, sl st in third ch from hook) twice, ch 3, sl st in center of next leaf; rep from * around, ending with (ch 6, sl st in third ch from hook) once, ch 1 and sl st in first ch made.

Row 3: Sc in same place as sl st. * Ch 8, sl st in third ch from hook, ch 5, trc in center st between next 2 picots, ch 5, sc in center st between next 2 picots. Rep from * around, join with sl st in first sc made. Fasten off. Starch lightly and press.

Crocheted Box Top

Shown on pages 114–115.

MATERIALS

Clark's Big Ball 3-Cord Crochet Cotton, Size 30: 1 ball white
Buttonhole twist thread, sewing threads, embroidery floss, and pearl cottons in various colors
Sizes 12 and 14 steel crochet hooks
Black taffeta fabric
Clear-drying fabric glue
Various beads, including rhinestones and pearls
Wooden box with recessed top
Quilt batting
18-inch gold braid

Abbreviations: Page 211.

INSTRUCTIONS

BASKET *Row 1:* With Size 30 thread and Size 12 hook, ch 4; work 9 dc in fourth ch from hook; ch 3, turn.

Row 2: Dc in first dc, (dc in next dc, 2 dc in next dc) 4 times; ch 3, turn (do not dc in turning ch).

Row 3: Dc in first dc and in next 2 dc, (2 dc in next dc, dc in next dc) 4 times; dc in each of next 2 dc, 2 dc in top of turning ch; ch 4, turn.

Row 4: Dc in first dc, * ch 1, dc in next dc; rep from * across; end ch 1, dc in top of turning ch; ch 5, turn.

Row 5: Trc in first dc, * ch 1, trc in next dc; rep from * across; end ch 1, trc in third ch of turning ch-4; ch 6, turn.

Row 6: Trc in first trc, * ch 2, trc in next trc; rep from * across; end ch 2, trc in fourth ch of turning ch-5; ch 4, turn.

Row 7: * 2 trc in ch-2 sp, trc in trc; rep from * across; end 2 trc in ch-6 turning sp; fasten off.

HANDLE *Row 1:* Ch 35. Sc in top lp of second ch and in top lp of each ch across; ch 1, turn.

Row 2: Sc in back lp of each sc across; fasten off.

STEMS: Mix 2 tablespoons white glue with 2 teaspoons water. Dip pieces of green embroidery floss into mixture; remove excess. Let dry and set aside.

LEAVES: Make a variety of leaves from embroidery floss and pearl cotton.

LEAF A: Ch 3, in third ch from hook work (dc, ch 2, dc, ch 2, and sl st); fasten off.

LEAF B: Ch 3, in third ch from hook work dc and trc; fasten off.

FLOWERS: Make a variety of flowers in various threads with Size 14 hook.

BELL-SHAPED FLOWER: Ch 3, in third ch from hook work 2 dc, ch 2, (in same ch work 2 dc, ch 2) 2 times; join with sl st to top of first dc; fasten off.

CUP-SHAPED FLOWER: Ch 2, in second ch from hook work *** sc, ch 1, dc, ch 1, sc—petal made;** rep from * twice more, working in the same ch; join with sl st to first sc at beg of rnd; fasten off. *Note:* Work additional reps to make slightly larger flower.

DAISY: Ch 3, dc in third ch from hook, ch 2, sl st in same ch, * ch 2, dc in same ch, ch 2, sl st in same ch; rep from * 3 times more; fasten off.

ROSE: Ch 24, in third ch from hook work (3 dc, ch 2, sl st in same ch), (sk next ch, sl st in next 2 ch, ch 2, 4 dc in same st as last sl st, ch 2, sl st in same ch) 3 times; (sk next ch, sl st in next 2 ch, ch 2, 5 dc in same st as last sl st, ch 2, sl st in same ch) twice; (sk next ch, sl st in next 2 ch, ch 2, 6 dc in same st as last sl st, ch 2, sl st in same ch) twice; fasten off.

ROSEBUD: Ch 3, in third ch from hook work (8 dc, ch 2, sl st in same ch); fasten off.

Dip flowers and leaves in diluted glue mixture. Shape petals and let dry on waxed paper. Roll strand of rose petals, beginning with smaller petals, to form shape; use straight pins to hold shape until dry.

ASSEMBLY: Mount taffeta in embroidery hoop. Center basket on fabric and tack in place with sewing thread. Loop handle and tack to center top of basket.

Arrange flowers and leaves in top of basket. Use stiffened embroidery floss (single, double, or triple plies) for stems. Glue and tack flowers in place as desired. Glue beads to flower centers.

Dip 6-strand embroidery floss into glue and shape bow; let dry. Glue bow to basket handle and add rhinestones as desired.

Cut cardboard circle the same size as recessed lid. Line with quilt batting and smooth taffeta over batting; trim edges. Secure taffeta to wrong side of cardboard and glue cardboard to lid. Trim with gold braid.

Crocheted Trinket Box

Shown on page 116.
The finished box measures 3x3x6 inches.

MATERIALS

DMC Cébélia Crochet Cotton, Size 30 (50-gram ball): 1 ball pale pink
Size 10 steel crochet hook
15x15-inch piece of illustration board
15x15-inch piece of polyester fleece
½ yard of blue fabric
White glue; small button
6 inches of narrow ribbon

Abbreviations: Page 211.
Gauge: 11 trc = 1 inch

INSTRUCTIONS

FRONT OF BOX: Ch 75.

Row 1: Trc in ninth ch from hook, * ch 2, sk 2 ch, trc in next ch; rep from * across—23 sps; ch 6, turn.

Row 2: Sk first sp, trc in next trc, * 2 trc in next sp, trc in next trc; rep from * across to last trc, ch 2, sk 2 ch, trc in third ch of ch-9; ch 6, turn.

Row 3: Sk sp, trc in first 19 trc, ch 15, sk 2 trc, trc in next 22 trc, ch 15, sk 2 trc, trc in last 19 trc, ch 2, trc in third ch of ch-6; ch 6, turn.

Row 4: (Trc in next 16 trc, ch 7, 2 sc over ch-15 lp, ch 7, sk 3 trc) twice, trc in last 16 trc, ch 2, trc in third ch of ch-6; ch 6, turn.

Row 5: Trc in first 13 trc, (ch 8, sc over ch-7 lp, sc in 2 sc, sc over next ch-7 lp, ch 8, sk 3 trc), trc in next 10 trc, repeat bet ( )s once more, trc in last 13 trc, ch 2, trc in third ch of ch-6; ch 6, turn.

Row 6: Trc in first 10 trc, (ch 10, sc over ch-8 lp, sc in 4 sc, sc over next ch-8 lp, ch 10, sk 3 trc), trc in next 4 trc; repeat bet ( )s once more, trc in last 10 trc, ch 2, trc in third ch of ch-6; ch 6, turn.

Row 7: Trc in first 10 trc, (3 trc over ch-10 lp, ch 9, sk 1 sc, sc in 4 sc, ch 9, 3 trc over ch-10 lp), trc in 4 trc, repeat bet ( )s once more, trc in last 10 trc, ch 2, trc in third ch of ch-6; ch 6, turn.

Row 8: Trc in 13 trc, (3 trc over ch-9 lp, ch 10, sk 1 sc, sc in 2 center sc, ch 10, 3 trc over ch-9 lp), trc in 10 trc, repeat bet ( )s once more, trc in last 13 trc, ch 2, trc in third ch of ch-6; ch 6, turn.

Row 9: (Trc in 16 trc, 3 trc over ch-10 lp, ch 2, 3 trc over next ch-10 lp) twice; trc in last 16 trc, ch 2, trc in third ch of ch-6; ch 6, turn.

Row 10: Trc in each trc across with 2 trc in each ch-2 sp of spiderwebs, ch 2, trc in third ch of ch-6; ch 6, turn.

Row 11: Trc in next trc, * ch 2, sk 2 trc, trc in next st; rep from * across; end trc in third ch of ch-6; ch 4, turn.

Row 12: * 2 trc in next sp, trc in next trc, rep from * across, trc in third ch of ch-6; ch 4, turn.

continued

BOTTOM OF BOX: *Rows 13–22:* Trc in each trc across and in top of turning ch; ch 4, turn. At end of Row 22, ch-6, turn.

BACK OF BOX: *Row 23:* * Sk 2 trc, trc in next trc, ch 2, rep from * across, end sk last 2 trc, trc in top of turning ch—23 sps; ch 6, turn.

Rows 24–33: Repeat rows 2–11. At end of Row 11, ch 6, turn.

LID OF BOX: *Row 34:* * Trc in next trc, ch 2, rep from * across; end trc in third ch of ch-6; ch 6, turn.

Rows 35–44: Rep Rows 2–11 once more, fasten off and do not ch 4 to turn at end of Row 44.

SIDES OF BOX: Attach thread at one corner of solid section that is bottom of box, ch 6. Working along side of solid section only, trc in end of next row, * ch 2, trc in end of next row, rep across to other solid corner—11 ch-2 sps; ch 6, turn.

Row 2: Sk first sp, trc in next trc, * 2 trc in next sp, trc in next trc; rep from * across to last trc, ch 2, sk 2 ch, trc in third ch of ch-6; ch 6, turn.

Row 3: Sk sp, trc in first 13 trc, ch 15, sk 2 trc, trc in last 13 trc, ch 2, trc in third ch of ch-6; ch 6, turn.

Rows 4–11: Same as rows 4–11 for front of box but make only 1 spiderweb. Fasten off and do not ch 4 to turn at end of Row 11.

Work other side section to correspond, but do not fasten off at end of Row 11. Working around outside edges of box, make 2 sc in each sp and 1 sc in each trc or row end and 5 sc in outer corners. Be careful to adjust tension so edge is firm but not too tight. Join to first sc; fasten off.

BLOCKING: Soak finished work in liquid starch solution or other stiffener. Pin out to dry, making rectangular sections 3x6 inches and end pieces 3x3 inches.

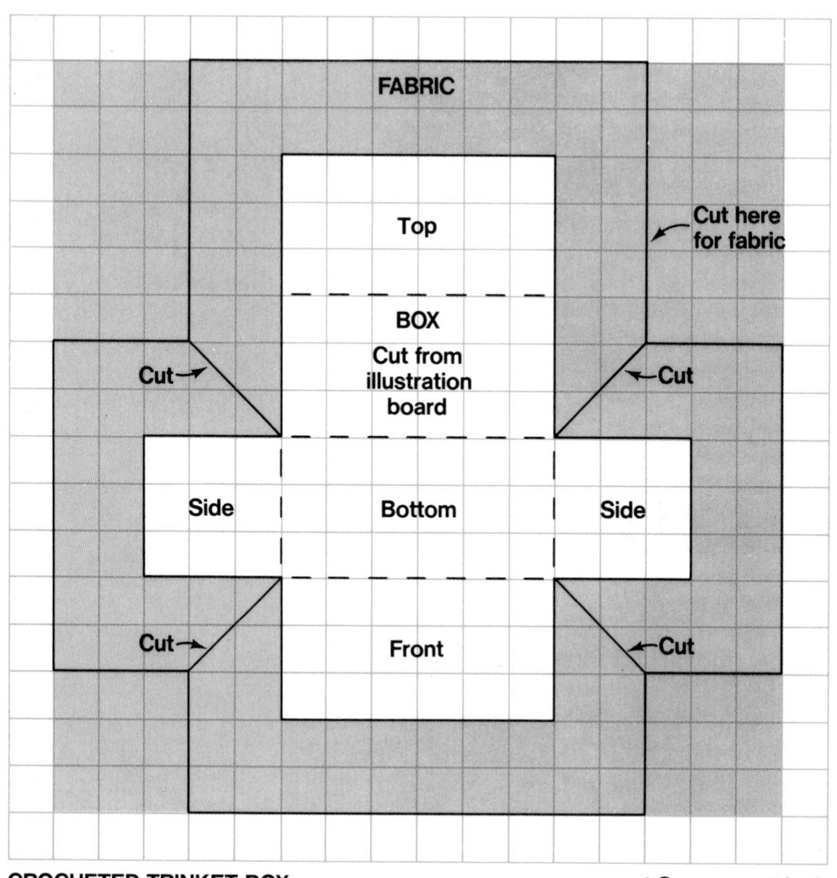

CROCHETED TRINKET BOX

1 Square = 1 Inch

FINISHING: Using the diagram, *above,* draw and cut box from illustration board using unshaded portion as pattern. With razor blade, *score* on dashed lines to make folding lines (score lines are on outside of box). Fold box, fit together, and trim away excess board (do not fasten together).

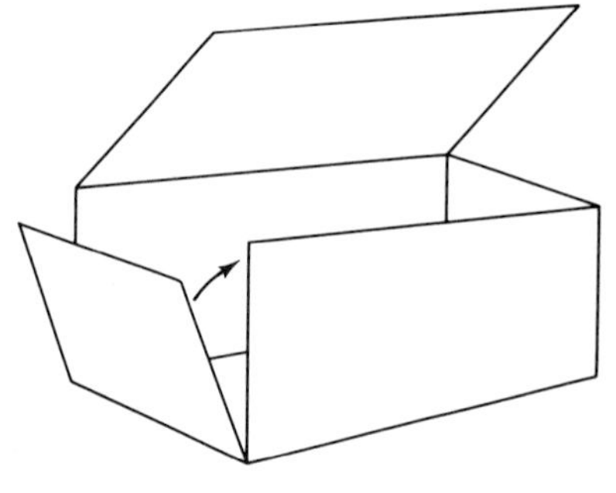

Lay flattened box on top of fabric, draw around leaving 2-inch margins (the shaded portion of box pattern); cut out fabric shape, slashing angles. Cut fleece same size as illustration board.

Glue fleece to illustration board on scored side. Fit fabric over box atop fleece, and glue margins to inside of box (trim away excess fabric); allow to dry. Tape box together on inside. Cut 3 pieces of blue fabric to fit bottom, lid, and sides of box for lining and glue in place.

Pin the crocheted piece to box, matching sides, and hand-sew together at sides; sew edges around top and lid to fabric. Loop ribbon, center, and tack to underside of lid; sew on button.

Large Crocheted Basket

Shown on page 117.
Bottom of basket is 5 inches in diameter.

MATERIALS
Phildar Perle Cotton, Size 5: 1 ball No. 88 pale peach
Size 8 steel crochet hook
White glue

Abbreviations: Page 211.
Gauge: 8 dc = 1 inch.

INSTRUCTIONS
Ch 6; join with sl st to form ring.

Rnd 1: Ch 3 (counts as first dc), 11 dc in ring; join with sl st to top of beg ch-3—12 dc, counting beg ch-3 as dc.

Rnds 2–3: Ch 3, dc in same st as join, make 2 dc in each dc around; join with sl st to top of ch-3—48 dc end of Rnd 3.

Rnd 4: Ch 1, sc in same st as join, (ch 3, sk 2 sts, sc in next st) 15 times; ch 3, sk 2 sts, join to sc at beg of rnd.

Rnd 5: Ch 11, sk next 2 ch-3 lps, dc in next sc, (ch 8, sk next 2 ch-3 lps, dc in next sc) 6 times; ch 8, join to third ch of ch-11—8 ch-8 lps.

Rnd 6: Ch 3, (11 dc in next ch-8 lp, dc in next dc) 7 times; 11 dc in last ch-8 lp; join to top of ch-3—96 dc.

Rnd 7: Ch 3, dc in each dc around; join to top of ch-3.

Rnd 8: Ch 6, * sk next 2 dc, sc in next dc, ch 3, sk next 2 dc, dc in next dc, ch 3; rep from * around; end sk 2 dc, join last ch-3 to third ch of beg ch-6—32 ch-3 lps.

Rnd 9: Ch 10, sk next 2 ch-3 lps, dc in next dc, * ch 7, sk next 2 ch-3 lps, dc in next dc; rep from * around; end ch 7, join to third ch of ch-10 at beg of rnd—16 ch-7 lps.

Rnd 10: Ch 3, * 8 dc in next ch-7 lp, dc in next dc, rep from * around; end 8 dc in last ch-7 lp; join to top of ch-3—144 dc.

Rnds 11–15: Ch 3, dc in each dc around; join to top of ch-3.

Rnd 16: Rep Rnd 8—48 ch-3 lps.

Rnd 17: Ch 9, rep Rnd 9, except ch 6 in lieu of ch 7; join to third ch of ch-9 at beg of rnd—24 ch-6 lps.

Rnd 18: Ch 3, * (6 dc in next ch-6 lp, dc in next dc) twice; 5 dc in next ch-6 lp; rep from * around; join to top of ch-3—160 dc.

Rnds 19–20: Ch 3, dc in each dc around; join to top of ch-3.

Rnd 21: Ch 1, sc in same st as join and next dc, * ch 5, sk next 2 dc, sc in next 2 dc; rep from * around; join to first sc—40 ch-5 lps.

Rnd 22: Sl st in next sc and next 2 chs, in same lp make 2 sc, * ch 7, 2 sc in next ch-5 lp; rep from * around; end ch 7, join to first sc.

Rnd 23: Sl st in next sc and next 2 ch, in same lp make 2 sc, ch 3, 2 sc; ch 1, * in next lp make 2 sc, ch 3, 2 sc; ch 1; rep from * around; end ch 1, join to first sc.

Note: Work double triple crochets (dtr) in next rnd, as follows: Yo hook 3 times, (yo, draw through 2 loops on hook) 4 times.

Rnd 24: Sl st in next sc and next ch, ch 4, trc in same lp, (ch 1, 2 trc in next ch-3 lp) twice, * ch 8, (dtr, ch 2, dtr) in next ch-3 lp, ch 8, (2 trc in next ch-3 lp, ch 1) twice, 2 trc in next ch-3 lp; rep from * around; end (dtr, ch 2, dtr) in next ch-3 lp, ch 8; join to top of ch-4; fasten off.

POINTS: *Row 1:* With right side facing, join thread in fourth ch of ch-8 lp *before* any dtr-group, ch 7, dtr in next dtr, ch 2, dtr in following dtr, ch 3, dtr in fifth ch of next ch-8 lp; turn.

Row 2: Ch 5, trc in dtr, ch 2, trc in next dtr, ch 2, trc in fourth ch of ch-8; turn.

Row 3: Ch 3, trc in next trc, ch 1, trc in next trc, ch 1, trc in third ch of ch-5. Fasten off.

Rep Rows 1–3 for rem 9 points.

EDGING: With right side facing, attach thread bet the center 2 trc bet points, ch 1, * sc bet same 2 trc. Working along edge of point, make 6 dc in first lp, 6 dc in second lp, 6 dc in third lp, and 6 dc in fourth lp, 1 dc bet the center 2 trc at top of point, (6 dc in next lp) 4 times. Rep from * around; join to first sc.

Next rnd: * Sc in each dc of next 6-dc grp, **ch 3, sl st to last sc made—picot made;** (dc in next dc, ch 2, sk next 2 sts, dc in next dc, make picot, ch 2, sk next 2 sts) twice; dc in next dc, ch 2, sk next 2 sts, (in next dc make dc, picot, dc; ch 2, sk next 2 sts) 3 times; (dc in next dc, make picot, ch 2, sk next 2 sts, dc in next dc, ch 2, sk next 2 sts) twice; dc in next dc, make picot, sc in each of next 6 dc of last 6-dc grp of point. Rep from * 9 times more; join to first sc. Fasten off.

FINISHING: Mix a solution of ⅔ glue to ⅓ water. Dip crochet into solution and stretch over an appropriate form until dry. See page 126 for tips for stiffening and shaping.

Small Crocheted Basket

Shown on page 117.
Basket is 4 inches in diameter and stands 4 inches tall.

MATERIALS
Phildar Pearl Cotton, Size 5: 1 ball No. 63 light blue
Size 8 steel crochet hook
White glue

Abbreviations: Page 211.
Gauge: 10 dc = 1 inch.

INSTRUCTIONS
Ch 6; join with sl st to form ring.

Rnd 1: Ch 3, make 15 dc in ring; sl st to top of ch-3 at beg of rnd—16 dc counting beg ch-3 as dc.

Rnd 2: Ch 4, dc in next dc, * ch 1, dc in next dc; rep from * around; end ch 1, join with sl st to third ch of ch-4.

continued

Rnd 3: Ch 3, * 2 dc in ch-2 sp, dc in next dc; rep from * around; end 2 dc in last ch-2 sp; join with sl st to top of ch-3—48 dc.

Rnd 4: Ch 5, * sk next dc, dc in next dc, ch 2; rep from * around; join last ch-2 with sl st to third ch of ch-5.

Rnd 5: Ch 3, 2 dc in next ch-2 sp, * dc in next dc, 2 dc in next ch-2 sp; rep from * around; join to top of ch-3—72 dc.

Rnd 6: Rep Rnd 4.

Rnd 7: Rep Rnd 5—108 dc.

Rnd 8: Ch 3, dc in next 5 dc, * 2 dc in next dc, dc in each of next 5 dc; rep from * around; join to top of ch-3—126 dc.

Rnd 9: Ch 3, dc around, inc 10 sts evenly spaced; join to top of ch-3—136 dc.

Rnds 10-11: Ch 3, dc in each dc around; join to top of ch-3.

Rnd 12: Ch 4, * sk next dc, dc in next dc, ch 1; rep from * around; join to third ch of ch-4.

Rnd 13: Ch 3, * dc in *each* ch-1 sp and dc around; join to top of ch-3—136 dc.

Rnd 14: Ch 4, (sk next dc, dc in next dc, ch 1) twice; sk next dc, dc in next 3 dc; * (ch 1, sk next dc, dc in next dc) 3 times; dc in next 2 dc; rep from * around; join to third ch of ch-4.

Rnd 15: Ch 3, * dc in next ch-1 sp, dc in next dc; ch 1, sk next ch-1 sp, dc in next dc, dc in ch-1 sp, dc in next dc, ch 1, sk next dc, dc in next dc; rep from * around; join to top of ch-3.

Rnd 16: Ch 4, sk next dc, dc in next dc, dc in next ch-1 sp, dc in next dc, ch 1, sk next dc, dc in next dc, * **in next sp make 5 dc, drop hook from lp, insert hook in top of first of 5 dc just made, draw dropped lp through—cluster (cl) made;** dc in next dc, ch 1, sk next st, dc in next dc, dc in next ch-1 sp, dc in next dc, ch 1, sk next st, dc in next dc; rep from * around; end with cl in last ch-1 sp, join to third ch of ch-4.

Rnd 17: Ch 3, * dc in next ch-1 sp, dc in next dc, ch 1, sk next dc, * dc in next dc, dc in ch-1 sp, dc in next dc, ch 1, sk next cl, dc in next dc; rep from * around; end ch 1, sk last cl; join to top of ch-3.

Rnd 18: Ch 4, * sk next st, dc in next dc, cl in next sp, dc in next dc, ch 1, sk next st, dc in next dc, dc in next sp, dc in next dc, ch 1; rep from * around; end dc in last dc, dc in ch-1 sp; join to third ch of ch-4.

Rnds 19–21: Work same as for Rnds 15, 16, and 17.

Rnd 22: Ch 4, * sk next dc, dc in next dc, ch 1, sk next ch-1 sp, dc in next dc, ch 1, sk next dc, dc in next dc and ch-1 sp and next dc, ch 1; rep from * around; end dc in last dc and ch-1 sp; join to third ch of ch-4.

Rnd 23: Ch 3, dc in *each* dc and ch-1 sp around; join to top of ch-3.

Rnd 24: Work same as for Rnd 12.

How To Stiffen and Shape Crocheted Baskets

The techniques you use to finish a crocheted basket are just as important as those you use to stitch it. Here are some tips to help you fashion crisp, symmetrical, and attractive containers once the crocheting is complete.

To begin, gather a piece of fiberboard, rust-proof pins, and aluminum foil or waxed paper. Then, consider the shape you want your basket to have. Your options are not restricted by the obvious shape of the crocheted piece. For example, the straight-side blue container, shown on page 117, could easily be shaped with a rolled-back edge along the top and the flared peach basket could be stiffened into a round container by shaping it over a small mixing bowl.

Next, find some "molds" with pleasing shapes—drinking glasses, mixing bowls, and vases, for example—and pull the basket around the different shapes before making a choice.

Keep in mind that the mold will be upside down while the basket dries, so you can achieve additional shapings. For example, if the mold is less deep than the basket, pin the rim of the basket to the fiberboard in a pleasing shape. Or, when the basket is dry, turn it right side up, and reshape the rim: Roll foil into a coil long enough to fit around the rim, then roll the basket edge around the coil; pin the crocheted edge to the foil and allow it to dry.

You can stiffen your basket with starch or glue, depending on whether you intend to launder it. If you plan to wash the basket, stiffen it with cooked starched. Follow the manufacturer's instructions for a very stiff finish.

If you do not intend to wash the basket, stiffen it by soaking it in a mixture of three parts white glue to one part water.

To protect a glue-stiffened basket from small amounts of moisture (so you can wipe it with a damp cloth), spray it lightly with several coats of clear, matte finish after the glue is completely dry.

Rnd 25: Work same as for Rnd 13.

Rnd 26: Ch 4, * sk next dc, dc in *each* of next 3 dc, ch 1; rep from * around; end dc in last 2 dc; join to third ch of ch-4.

POINTS: *Row 1:* Ch 2 for first dc, * dc in next sp, dc in next dc, ch 1, sk next st, dc in next dc, cl in next sp, dc in next dc, ch 1, sk next st, dc in next dc; *turn.*

Row 2: Sl st to ch-1 sp, ch 2 (counts as first dc), dc in next dc, ch 2, sk cl, dc in next dc, dc in next sp, dc in next dc; *turn.*

Row 3: * Sl st to third dc, ch 2, dc in sp, ch 2; sl st in top of next dc; then sl st along rem left edge of point to top of last dc of Row 1; rep from * 17 times; fasten off.

FINISHING: Complete as for Large Crocheted Basket, page 125.

Linen Doily with Crocheted Edges

Shown on page 117.
Finished size is 13x13 inches.

MATERIALS

Clark's Big Ball 3-Cord Crochet Cotton, Size 30 (500-yard ball): 1 ball of No. 1 white
Size 10 steel crochet hook
White linen handkerchief

Abbreviations: Page 211.

INSTRUCTIONS

MOTIF (make 4): Beg at center, ch 8; join with sl st to form ring.

Row 1: Ch 6; in ring make (dc, ch 3) 4 times; dc in ring—5 ch-3 lps; do not join; ch 3, turn.

Row 2: Make 5 dc in first ch-3 sp, (make 6 dc in next ch-3 sp) 4 times—30 dc, counting ch-3 as 1 dc; ch 3, turn.

Row 3: Dc in next dc and in each dc across, dc in top of ch-3; ch 4, turn.

Row 4: (Dc in next dc, ch 1) 28 times; dc in top of ch-3; ch 1, turn.

Row 5: Sc in first ch-1 sp; (ch 6, sk next sp, sc in next sp) 13 times; ch 3, sk next sp and next dc, dc in ch-4 lp—14 lps; ch 6, turn.

Row 6: (Sc in next lp, ch 6) 11 times; sc in next lp, ch 3, dc in last lp—13 lps; ch 6, turn.

Row 7: (Sc in next lp, ch 6) 10 times; sc in last lp—12 lps; ch 3, turn.

Row 8: Make 5 dc in first lp, (6 dc in next lp) 11 times—72 dc, counting ch-3 as 1 dc; ch 3, turn.

Row 9: Dc in next dc and in each dc across, dc in top of ch-3; ch 3, turn.

Row 10: Dc in next dc and in each dc across, dc in top of ch-3; ch 4, turn.

Row 11: * Dc in next dc, ch 1. Rep from * across, ending with dc in top of ch-3; ch 7, turn.

Row 12: Sk first ch-1 sp, sc in next sp, (ch 7, sk next 2 sps, sc in next sp) 23 times; ch 4, dc in third ch from hook—1 sp inc'd; ch 7, turn—25 lps.

Row 13: Sc in next lp, (ch 7, sc in next lp) 22 times; ch 4, dc in last lp; ch 7, turn—24 lps.

Row 14: Sc in next lp, (ch 7, sc in next lp) 21 times; ch 4, dc in last lp; ch 4, turn.

Row 15: In first lp make (2 trc, ch 2 and 3 trc); * ch 6, sk next lp; in next lp make **3 trc, ch 2, 3 trc—shell made;** rep from * across; ch 4, turn—12 shells made.

Row 16: **In ch-2 sp of next shell make 3 trc, ch 2, 3 trc—shell over shell made;** * ch 3, sc in next ch-6 lp, ch 3, shell over shell; rep from * across; trc in top of ch-4; ch 4, turn.

Row 17: Shell over shell, * ch 7, shell over shell; rep from * across, trc in top of ch-4; ch 4, turn.

Row 18: Shell over shell, * ch 4, sc in ch-7 sp, ch 4, shell over shell; rep from * across; trc in top of ch-4; ch 4, turn.

Row 19: Shell over shell, * ch 8, shell over shell; rep from * across; trc in top of ch-4; ch 4, turn.

Row 20: * In sp of next shell make (trc, **ch 3, sl st in 3rd ch from hook—picot made**) 6 times; trc in same sp; ch 4, sc in ch-8 lp, ch 4; rep from * across, making in sp of last shell (trc and picot) 6 times; trc in same sp; trc in top of ch-4; fasten off.

Block pieces. Finish edges of handkerchief to same size as straight edges of edging pieces. Sew each motif to one side of square.

Crocheted Sachets

Shown on page 117.

MATERIALS

DMC Pearl Cotton, Size 5 (53-yard balls): 1 ball for 1 sachet
Size 4 steel crochet hook
Potpourri
Purchased appliqués
White glue

Abbreviations: Page 211.
Gauge: 7 dc = 1 inch.

INSTRUCTIONS

Ch 21. *Row 1:* Sc in second ch from hook and in each ch across—20 sc; ch 1, turn.

Row 2: Sc in first sc and in each sc across. Rep Row 2 for a total of 43 rows; do not fasten off.

Fold work in half to form square. Sc evenly around 4 sides, (to include folded edge), through both thicknesses working 1 sc in each sc or end of row and 1 sc in corner. Before completing fourth side, fill square with potpourri and sc closed; do not fasten off.

EDGING: *Rnd 1:* (Ch 3, 2 dc, ch 2, 3 dc) in first sc, sk 2 sc, * in next sc work (3 dc, ch 2, 3 dc)—shell made, sk 2 sc; rep from * around; join to top of ch-3.

Rnd 2: Sl st in next 2 dc and into ch-2 sp; work shell in each shell around; fasten off.

Glue an Glue an appliqué to one corner of sachet.

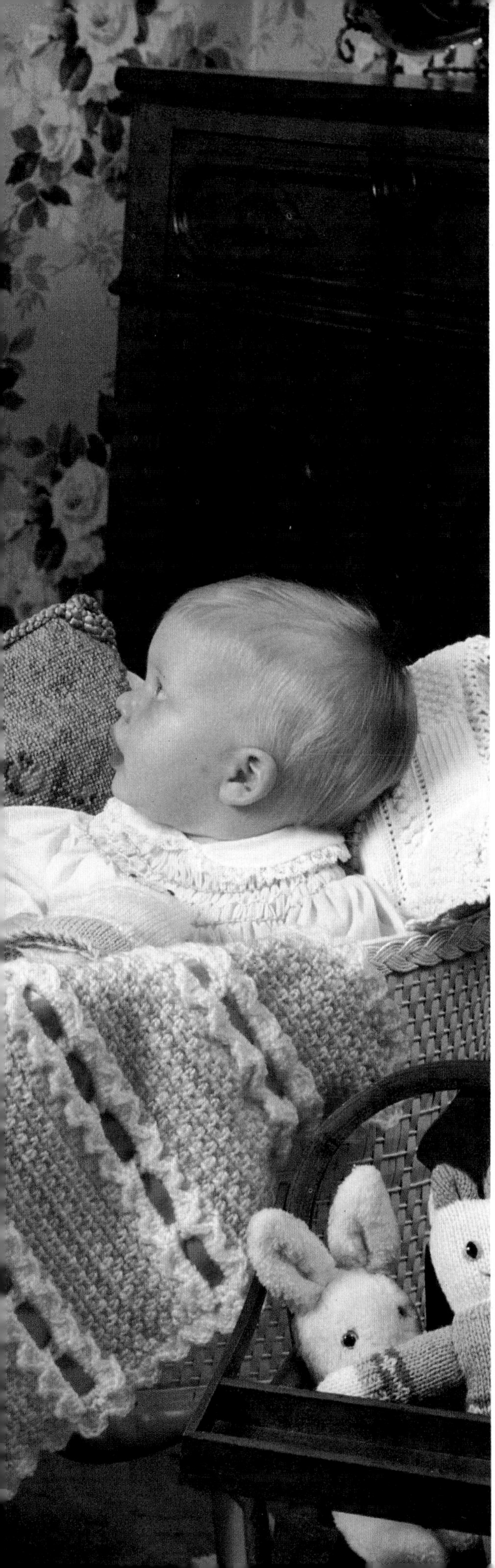

Petite Treasures

ENCHANTING GIFTS FOR CHILDREN

If you're searching for an extra-special gift to make for an infant or an older child, you'll surely find your heart's desire among the charming, one-of-a-kind designs in this chapter.

There's an old-fashioned air about the beribboned blanket, *left,* that seems made to order for an antique cradle or basinette. Yet, thanks to easy-care yarns and trims, modern moms can breath easy when it comes time to clean this coverlet.

Washable materials also are a must for the winsome pair of knitted kittens, *above.* One or the other of these tiny toys might be the perfect choice for a newborn's first (and soon-to-be-favorite) crib toy. Directions for these projects begin on page 140.

ENCHANTING GIFTS FOR CHILDREN

A kitten, a bear, and a buffalo are just a few of the 17 silhouettes to be found in the colorful menagerie shown on these pages. Choose your favorites among the animals to stitch into a coverlet, picture, pillow, or other fanciful projects to dress up your own baby's nursery or that of a friend or loved one.

All of the designs are included in the crocheted and quilted throw, *opposite.* To make your own version of this 30x35-inch coverlet, stitch the animal blocks in rainbow hues of pearl cotton threads. Set them together with white blocks that feature a simple geometric motif.

To complete the coverlet and display the lacy blocks to advantage, tack the crocheted top over a pastel quilt edged with a multicolored ruffle.

A crouching hare is delightfully apparent in the framed picture, *above left.* Worked in dark pearl cotton, the design clearly shows against a muslin backing. You can stitch and frame any of the motifs in a similar fashion.

A robin, a camel, a duck, and an elephant meet together on the ruffled pillow, *left.* When assembling this project, be sure to flop two of the patterns so the animals seem to be facing each other in pairs on the pillow front.

ENCHANTING GIFTS FOR CHILDREN

Destined to become an instant heirloom, this dainty christening ensemble makes an exceptionally thoughtful baby gift—one that surely will be treasured for generations to come.

Both the dress and matching cap are worked primarily in a graceful shell stitch pattern using lustrous pearl cotton thread.

Simple embroidery and a scattering of purchased floral appliqués are set atop bands of single crochet at the yoke and hem of the dress. A lacy border and three insertion rows of satin ribbon complete the accents. Single florets and a spill of ribbons trim the bonnet.

This lovely ensemble might be a godmother's special gift to her godchild. Or a doting grandmother might choose to make a christening set for each of her grandchildren. You can alter the colors of the ribbons and appliqués to personalize the gown for each and every child.

ENCHANTING GIFTS FOR CHILDREN

Carry a new baby home from the hospital or off to Grandmother's house in this cozy, quilt-stitch bunting and blanket set. Knitted with sport yarn on Size 2 needles, this intriguing pattern lends a softly sculptured texture to the knitted surface, creating a design that appears to be quilted in tiny diamonds.

Here we show the bunting in a soft shade of pink, and the blanket in a lovely combination of ice blue, pink, and raspberry. Soft yellow accented with peach and aqua or spring green makes another pretty color combination.

Directions are given for sizes newborn to six months and six months to one year.

ENCHANTING GIFTS FOR CHILDREN

Any one of these charming collars makes a party-time touch for a child's simple cotton frock. The dress might be ready-made or one you've stitched up yourself with just such a collar in mind.

Pictured at near right is a lacy Peter Pan collar designed to slip over or under the smaller fabric collar on a dress or blouse. In wintertime, the same collar works equally well over a collarless sweater or wool dress.

The birthday girl, *opposite,* center right and *below,* sports a snappy crocheted sailor collar with a gently scalloped edge. This design fits neatly inside a V-neckline jumper or dress. Purchased floral appliqués embellish each corner of the back flap.

Our third party goer, *opposite,* far right, shows off an openwork collar that has been sewn to the yoke of her dress. The lacing of satin ribbon at the neck is a festive, feminine finishing touch.

All three collars transfer easily from one garment to another and each could dress up a number of different items in your child's wardrobe.

ENCHANTING GIFTS FOR CHILDREN

Whatever the season, active kids need sweaters that are fun to wear and a snap to take care of. The designs on these pages are sized for tiny tots and bigger kids too—and both designs make great additions to any child's wardrobe.

The classic fleck-pattern pullover, *left* and *below,* sports a flock of sheep ambling around the waist and cuffs. Bright, breezy colors in washable, sport yarn give this sweater a contemporary look for little girls. You may want to choose more traditional shades for the guys in your family.

FILET CROCHET ANIMAL COVERLET AND PILLOW

■ Block (bl) □ Space (sp)

ENCHANTING GIFTS FOR CHILDREN

With right sides facing, sew short ends of peach strips, making a tube; press seams open. Fold tube in half, wrong sides facing and raw edges even; gather along the ½-inch seam line, to fit outside edges of top piece. Repeat for other 2 colors of chintz. With right sides facing, baste the blue, yellow, then peach ruffles to the blue top piece; sew through all layers.

Baste quilt batting to wrong side of backing. With right sides facing, sew top and back together (pin ruffles to top piece to avoid catching in seams); leave an opening for turning. Clip seams, turn, press, and sew opening closed. Remove basting threads; hand-sew the crocheted piece to the top along outside edges; then tack through all layers at intersections of the blocks.

To make the pillow

Make four animal blocks of your choice, using instructions for coverlet, page 142.

Next, from blue chintz, cut pillow top and back, making them 1 inch larger than assembled animal blocks to allow for ½-inch seam allowance. Cover cotton cording with blue chintz and baste to one of blue pieces for top.

Cutting strips to measure twice the perimeter of pillow, cut 7-inch-wide strips of peach for outside ruffle and 6-inch-wide strips of yellow for inside ruffle; gather to fit top piece. With right sides facing, sew ruffles into place. Sew back to front, right sides facing, leaving an opening for turning; clip seams, turn, and press. Sew crocheted piece atop and stuff; sew opening closed.

Crocheted Christening Gown And Bonnet

Shown on pages 132–133. Finished size is for 3- to 6-month-old baby.

MATERIALS

Phildar Pearl Cotton, Size 5 (40-gram balls): 12 balls
Size 0 steel crochet hook
Three ¼-inch-diameter buttons
Embroidery floss
Purchased appliqués
5 yards of ⅜-inch satin ribbon
Water-erasable pen

Abbreviations: Page 211.
Gauge: 2 shells in pat = 1¾ inches.

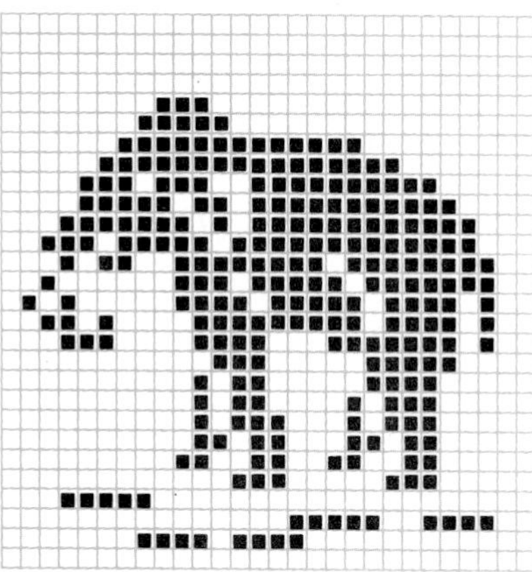
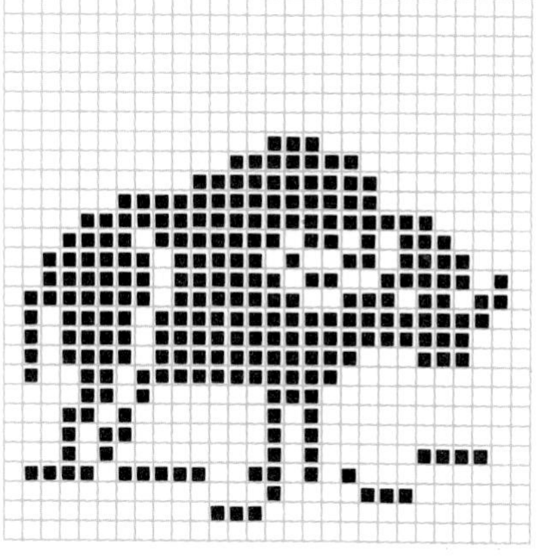
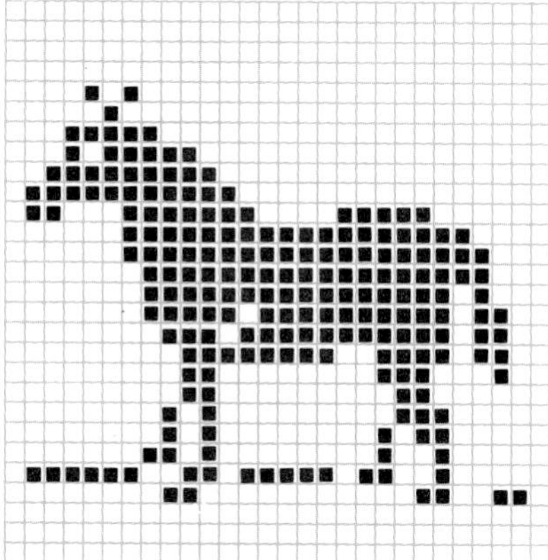
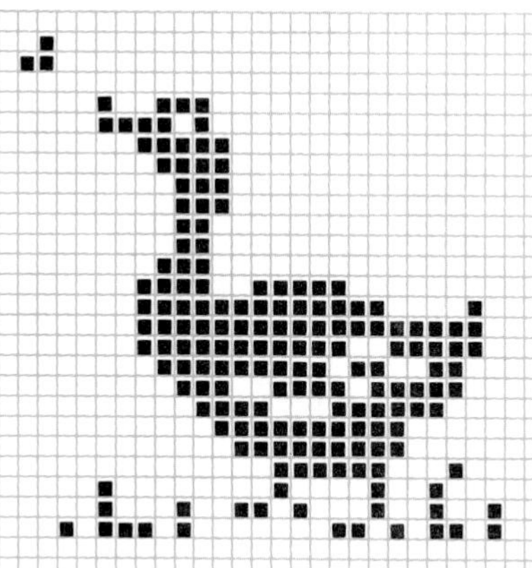
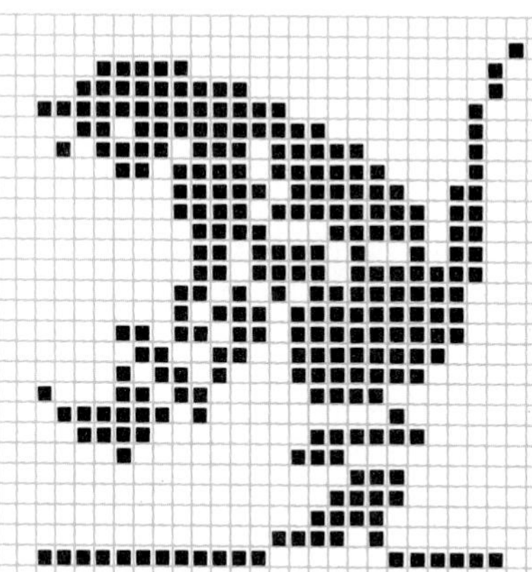
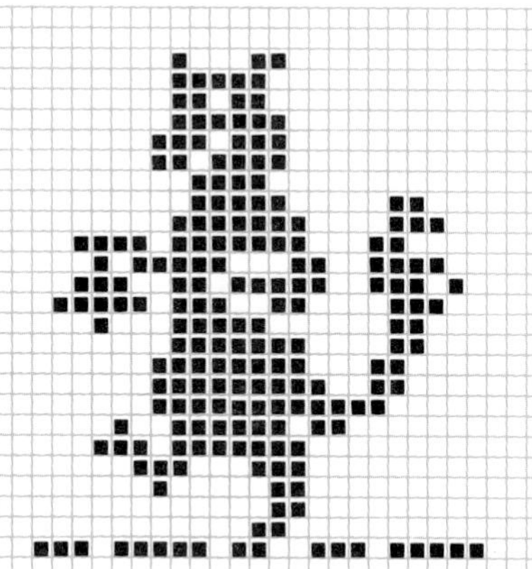

FILET CROCHET ANIMAL COVERLET AND PILLOW

■ Block (bl) □ Space (sp)

INSTRUCTIONS
For the dress

Beg at neck edge, ch 77; do not join.

Row 1: Working in top lps, sc in second ch from hook and in each of next 12 ch, 3 sc in next ch—for seam; sc in next 11 ch—sleeve; 3 sc in next ch—seam; sc in next 24 ch—front; 3 sc in next ch—seam; sc in next 11 ch—sleeve; 3 sc in next ch-seam; sc in last 13 ch—84 sc across; ch 1, turn.

Row 2: Working in back lps, * sc in each sc to center sc of next 3-sc grp, 3 sc in center sc; rep from * 3 times more, sc in each sc to end of row—8 sc increased; ch 1, turn.

Rows 3-13: Rep Row 2—180 sc at end of Row 13; ch 3, turn.

YOKE EXTENSIONS FOR BACK: *Row 14:* Working under both lps, dc in next sc, (ch 1, sk sc, dc in next sc) 12 times, dc in next sc, ch 1, turn—12 ch-1 sps.

Row 15 (right side): Sc in first 2 dc, * sc in ch-1 sp, sc in next dc; rep from * across, end sc in top of ch-3—27 sc; fasten off.

Join thread on wrong side in center sc along *armhole* edge of rem back yoke piece, ch 3; rep Rows 14–15; fasten off.

YOKE EXTENSIONS FOR THE FRONT: *Row 14:* With wrong side facing, join thread in center sc along *armhole* edge of front piece, ch 3 and working under both lps, dc in next sc, (ch 1, sk sc, dc in next sc) 24 times, dc in next sc, ch 1, turn—24 ch-1 sps.

Row 15: Rep Row 15 of yoke extension for Back—51 sc; do not fasten off; do not turn.

Row 16 (joining fronts and back together): Ch 3, sc in first sc of Row 15 of back yoke, sc in next 7 sc, 2 sc in each sc across this piece to within last 2 sts, overlap the last 2 sc of this yoke piece over the first 2 sc of next back yoke piece and working through *both* thicknesses, work 2 sc in each of these 2 sts—back yoke pieces joined; 2 sc in each sc of rem back yoke piece until 8 sts rem; sc in each sc to end; ch 3, sc in first sc of Row 15 along front yoke piece and in next 7 sc, 2 sc in each sc to last 8 sc, sc in each sc to end of row—174 sts around.

BEGIN SKIRT: *Rnd 1:* Ch 3, dc in each sc around, working 4 dc in ch-3 lps at underarms—182 dc around; join with sc in top of ch-3 at beg of rnd.

Rnd 2: Sk next dc, * 5 dc in *back* lp of next dc, sk dc, sc in *back* lp of next dc, sk next dc; rep from * around—45 shell-grps made; do not join.

Rnd 3: * Sc in *back* lp of center dc of next 5-dc grp, 5 dc in *back* lp of next sc; rep from * around; do not join.

Rep Rnd 3 for 36 more rnds; end with either sc or 5 dc-shell to complete last rnd.

INSERTION: *Rnd 1:* Work sc in *back* lp of each dc *and* hdc in back lp of each sc around; join with sl st to first st.

Rnd 2: Ch 5, * sk 2 sts, dc in next st, ch 2, rep from * around; join with sl st to third ch of ch-5 at beg of rnd.

Rnd 3: Ch 1, sc in same st as join; * 2 sc in ch-2 sp, sc in next dc; rep from * around; join with sl st in *back* lp of first sc.

APPLIQUÉD BORDER STRIP: *Rnd 1:* Ch 1, sc in same st as join; sc in *back* lp of each sc around; join with sl st in *back* lp of first sc.

Rep Rnd 1 for 19 more rnds or for 3½ inches.

Rep rnds 2-3 of Insertion; join last rnd with sl st to first sc under both lps.

Next rnd: Ch 3, dc in each dc around; join with sl st to top of ch-3.

Following rnd: Ch 4, * sk dc, dc in next dc, ch 1; rep from * around; join with sl st to third ch of ch-4.

BORDER: *Rnd 1:* Sl st in next ch-1 sp, ch 3, in same sp work dc, ch 2, 2 dc; * ch 1, sc in next ch-1 sp, ch 1, in next ch-1 sp work **2 dc, ch 2, 2 dc—shell made;** rep from * around; end ch 1, sl st to top of ch-3.

Rnd 2: Ch 3, dc in next dc; shell in next ch-2 sp, * dc in next 2 dc, ch 2, sc in ch-2 sp of next shell, ch 2, dc in first 2 dc of next shell, shell in ch-2 sp of shell; rep from * around; join last ch-2 to top of ch-3.

Rnd 3: Ch 3, dc in next 3 dc, * shell in ch-2 sp of next shell; dc in next 4 dc; sk next 2 ch-2 lps, dc in next 4 dc; rep from * around; join to top of ch-3.

Rnd 4: Sl st in next dc, ch 3, dc in next 4 dc; * in ch-2 sp of shell work (dc, **ch 3, sl st in third ch from hook—picot made,** and dc); dc in next 5 dc, ch 3, make picot, sk next 2 dc, dc in next 5 dc; rep from * around; end with picot; join to top of ch-3; fasten off.

NECKLINE FINISHING: With the right side facing, join thread at lower left Back opening just above placement for ribbon and work 14 sc to top of neck edge; sc in next 12 sc across back neck edge; (draw up lp in next sc, sk next st, draw up lp in next sc, yo, draw through 3 lps on hook), sc in next 9 sc; rep between ( )s; sc in next 22 sc: rep between ( )s; sc in next 9 sc; rep between ( )s; sc in 12 sc across back; work 14 sc down neck opening; fasten off.

Next row: Join thread in first sc of previous row, ch 1, sc in same st, sc in next sc (ch 4, sc in next 5 sc) twice; ch 4, sc in next 3 sc; in each st around neck edge work (sc, ch 1, sc); sc in each sc down back opening; fasten off.

SLEEVES: *Rnd 1:* With right side facing, join thread at underarm, work 48 sc evenly spaced around armhole opening; join with sl st to first sc.

Rnd 2: Ch 1, sc in same st as join and next 7 sc, [sk sc, 5 dc in *back* lp of next sc, sk sc, sc in *back* lp of next sc] twice ; (5 dc in next sc, sc in next sc) 9 times; rep bet [ ]s twice; working under both lps, sc in last 5 sc; join to first sc.

continued

Rnd 3: Ch 1, sc in same st as join and next 7 sc; (sc in *back* lp of center st of 5-dc grp, 5 dc in *back* lp of sc) 12 times, sc in top of next 5 dc-grp, sc in next 6 sc (under both lps); join to first sc.

Rnd 4: Ch 1, sc in same st as join and next 8 sc; (sc in *back* lp of center st of 5-dc grp; 5 dc in *back* lp of next sc) 11 times; sc in top of next 5-dc grp; sc in next 7 sc (under both lps); join to first sc.

Rnd 5: Ch 1, sc in same st as join and next 8 sc; (5 dc in *back* lp of next sc, sc in top of next 5-dc grp) 12 times, sk next sc; sc under both lps of next sc, ch 2, *turn.*

Note: To work dc decrease in next 2 rnds, work as follows: yo, draw up lp in dc, yo, draw through 2 lps on hook, yo, draw up lp in next dc, yo draw through 2 lps on hook, yo, draw through 3 lps on hook.

Rnd 6: Sk first st, (work dc dec over next 2 sts) 36 times; ch 2, *turn.*

Rnd 7: Sk first st, (work dc dec over next 2 sts) 17 times; work dec over next 2 turning lps, sc in next 5 sc, join.

Note: To work sc decrease in next rnd, work as follows; draw up lp in each of next 2 sts, yo, draw through 3 lps on hook.

Rnd 8: Ch 1, sc in same st as join, sc in *back* lp of next 7 sc, work sc-dec over next 2 turning ch-lp, sc in next sc, (sc-dec over next 2 sts, sc in next st) 6 times, sc in *back* lp of next 5 sc; join to first sc.

Rnd 9–11: Work sc in *back* lp of each st around; do not join rnds.

Rnd 12: Working under both lps, in each st around work (sc, ch 1, sc); fasten off.

FINISHING: With water-erasable pen, draw wavy lines around appliqué strip. Embroider line with outline stitches using 3 strands of floss. Arrange appliqués around the wavy line (refer to photograph for guide) and sew in place. Using lazy-daisy stitches with two strands of floss, embroider leaves to fill in the spaces. Sew three appliqués to yoke of dress. Weave ribbons through insertion strips on skirt and yoke; tack in place. Sew buttons at neck opening.

For the bonnet

Beg at back of neck, ch 40.

Row 1: Sc in second ch and each ch across—39 sc; ch 1, turn.

Row 2: * Sc in each of next 2 sc, 2 sc in next sc; rep from * across, end sc in last sc, ch 1, turn.

Row 3: Sc in each sc across—51 sc; ch 1, turn.

Row 4: Rep Row 2.

Rows 5–6: Rep Row 3.

Row 7: Sc in 20 sc, 2 sc in next sc; (sc in 5 sc, 2 sc in next sc) 3 times; sc in next 13 sc; sl st in next sc; ch 1, turn.

Row 8: Sk sl st, sc in next sc and next 41 sc; sl st in next sc; ch 1, turn.

Row 9: Sk sl st, (sc in next 10 sc, 2 sc in next sc) 3 times; sc in 8 sc, sc in same st as sl st in Row 7, sc in next 2 sc, sl st in next sc, ch 1, turn.

Row 10: Sk sl st, (sc in next 8 sc, 2 sc in next sc) 4 times, sc in 11 sc, sc in same st as sl st in Row 8, sc in next 2 sc, sl st in next sc, ch 1, turn.

Row 11: Sk sl st, sc in 54 sc, sc in same st as sl st in Row 9, sc in 4 sc, sl st in next sc, ch 1, turn.

Row 12: Sk sl st, sc in each sc across, sc in same st as sl st in Row 10, sc in next 4 sc, sl st in next sc; ch 1, turn.

Row 13: Sk sl st (sc in next 15 sc, 2 sc in next sc) 3 times, sc in next 17 sc, sc in same st as sl st in Row 11, sc in each sc to end of row; ch 1, turn.

Row 14: Sc in each sc across, sc in same st as sl st in Row 12, sc in each sc to end of row; ch 1, turn.

Row 15: Sc in first sc, * sk 2 sc, 5 dc in *back* lp of next sc, sk 2 sc, sc in *back* lp of next sc; rep from * across row, end 3 dc in *back* lp of last sc; fasten off.

Row 16: Join thread in sc at beg of Row 15, ch 3, 2 dc in same st, * sc in *back* lp of center dc of 5-dc grp, 5 dc in *back* lp of next sc; rep from * across, end sc in top of last dc; fasten off.

Row 17: Join thread in top of ch-3 at beg of Row 16; sc in same st, work in 5-dc pat across; fasten off.

Rep Rows 16–17 three times more, then rep Row 16; tie in all ends.

Rnd 18: Working around 2 sides and back edge, work sc evenly spaced around, working 3 sc in corners, ch 1, turn.

Rnd 19: In each st around the next 3 sides work (sc, ch 1, sc); fasten off.

FINISHING: Tack ribbons at back edges to tie at nape of neck; tack ribbons at side edges to tie under chin, and sew appliqués atop the chin ribbons.

Knitted Quilt Stitch Bunting And Blanket

Shown on pages 134–135.

Directions are for newborn to six months. Changes for size six months to one year follow in parentheses. Finished chest measures 22 (24½) inches. Blanket is approximately 39x43½ inches.

MATERIALS

For the bunting

Unger Roly Sport Yarn (1¾-ounce balls): 7 (8) skeins pink
Size 2 knitting needles
22-inch zipper
Stitch markers

For the blanket

Unger Roly Sport Yarn (1¾-ounce skeins): 7 skeins ice blue, 3 skeins pink, 2 skeins raspberry
Size 3 circular knitting needle, 29 inches long
2 stitch markers

Abbreviations: Page 217.
Gauge: For the bunting, over pat st, 27 sts = 4 inches.

For the blanket, over pat st 23 sts = 4 inches; 45 rows = 4 inches.

INSTRUCTIONS

QUILT PATTERN (multiple of 4 sts plus 3): *Row 1* (wrong side): Purl.

Rows 2-5: Work in stockinette st (k one row, p row alternately).

Row 6 (right side): K 3, * [sl next st off needle and ravel for 4 rows, insert right needle into dropped st and under 4 threads and k this st (4 threads will lie on top of yarn coming from st just knit)]; k 3; rep from * across.

Rows 7-11: Rep Rows 1-5.

Row 12: K 1, * rep bet [ ]s of Row 6, k 3; rep from * across to last 2 sts; end rep bet [ ]s of Row 6, k 1.

Rep Rows 1-12 for pat.

Note: When shaping, continue to drop st as indicated in pat as long as there is at least 1 st bet dropped st and edge.

For the bunting

BODY: Cast on 149 (165) sts for lower edge. Work in garter st (knit every row) for 6 rows.

Next row (wrong side): Keeping first 5 sts and last 5 sts in garter st, work rem 139 (155) sts in Row 1 of quilt pat. Continue in quilt pat until total length measures 15½ (18½) inches; ending with Row 6 of quilt pat.

DIVIDE FOR FRONTS AND BACK: With wrong side facing and keeping to garter st and quilt pat as established, work 40 (44) sts and sl to holder for Left Front. Bind off 1 st for underarm, work 67 (75) sts in pat for Back; sl rem 41 (45) sts to holder for underarm and Right Front.

BACK: *Next row:* Keeping to pat as established, work raglan shaping on 67 (75) sts of Back as follows: *Row 1:* K 1, sl 1, k 1, psso, work to last 3 sts, k 2 tog, k 1—65 (73) sts.

Row 2: Work even in pat.

Row 3: Rep Row 1—63 (71) sts.

Rows 4-6: Work even in pat.

Rep these 6 rows 10 (11) times more for raglan dec ending with Row 1 (7) of quilt pat. Sl rem 23 (27) sts to holder for Back neck ribbing. Break off.

LEFT FRONT: Sl 40 (44) sts of Left Front from holder to needle. With right side facing, join yarn at armhole and keeping to garter st and quilt pat as established, work raglan dec at armhole edge as follows: *Row 1:* K 1, sl 1, k 1, psso, work across in pat—39 (43) sts.

Row 2: Work even.

Row 3: Rep Row 1—38 (42) sts.

Rows 4-6: Work even in pats.

Rep these 6 rows 10 (11) times more, ending with Row 1 (7) of quilt pat. Sl rem 18 (20) sts to holder for neck ribbing. Break off.

RIGHT FRONT: Sl 41 (45) sts of Right Front to needle. Join yarn at underarm. With wrong side facing and keeping to quilt and garter pat as established, bind off 1 st for underarm, work in pat to end of row—40 (44) sts.

Work raglan dec at armhole edge as follows: *Row 1* (right side): Work in pat to within last 3 sts, k 2 tog, k 1. Continue to work raglan shaping to correspond to Left Front, ending with Row 1 (7) of quilt pat. Sl rem 18 (20) sts to holder for right Front neck ribbing. Break off.

LEFT SLEEVE (starting with mitten end): *Both sizes:* Cast on 19 stitches. K 5 rows for garter st cuff.

Next row (wrong side): P.

Continue in st st (k one row, p one row) for 18 rows more, ending with a p row.

Dec for tip of mitten, Row 1: K 1, k 2 tog, k 13, k 2 tog through back lps (tbl), k 1—17 sts.

Row 2: P.

Row 3: K 1, k 2 tog, k 11, k 2 tbl, k 1—15 sts.

Next row: K (to form ridge on right side for fold line).

Following row (back of mitten): Beg with Row 2 of quilt pat and inc as follows: *Row 1:* Inc 1 st each end—17 sts.

Row 2: Work even.

Row 3: Inc 1 st each end—19 sts.

Rows 4-5: Work even in pat.

Keeping to pat as established, work even for 18 rows ending with Row 12 of quilt pat.

Next row: Cast on 24 sts at beg of row, complete row in pat—43 sts.

Keeping to pat over 19 sts, work rem 24 (24) sts in garter st for next 5 rows ending with Row 6 of quilt pat over first 19 sts.

Next row: K 1, p 18, k to end of row (garter st cuff).

Working all 43 (43) sts in quilt pat, work even for 22 (22) rows ending with Row 4 of quilt pat.

SLEEVE SHAPING: Inc 1 st at beg and end of row—45 sts. Keeping to pat, rep inc row every 12th row 3 (5) times, working added sts in quilt pat (see note following quilt pat above)—51 (55) sts.

Work even until length from second garter st cuff (cuff following 24-st cast on) measures approximately 6½ (8¼) inches, end with Row 12 of quilt pat.

Inc 1 st each end on next row, then every other row twice more ending with Row 5 of quilt pat—57 (61) sts.

TOP SHAPING: Keeping to pat, bind off 1 st at beg of next 2 rows—55 (59) sts.

Keeping to pat, work raglan shaping as for Back and rep 6-row dec-shaping 11 (12) times ending with Row 1 (7) of quilt pat. Sl rem 11 sts to holder for neck ribbing. Break off.

RIGHT SLEEVE: Rep as for Left Sleeve, reversing shaping.

FINISHING: Sew side seams of mitten, taking care to overlap garter st cuffs placing quilt-st-cuff over st-st-cuff. Sew raglan and sleeve seams.

continued

NECK RIBBING: Sl 18 (20) sts of Left Front to needle, then sl 11 Left Sleeve sts, 23 (27) Back sts, 11 Right Sleeve sts and 18 (20) sts of Right Front to same needle—81 (89) sts.

With right side facing, join yarn at right Front edge, k 10 (12), * inc 1 st in next st, k 3, inc 1 st in next st *, k 2, k 2 tog, k 9, k 2 tog, k 6, inc 1 st in next st, k 7 (11), inc 1 st in next st, k 6, k 2 tog, k 9, k 2 tog, k 2, rep bet *s once; k 10 (12)—83 (91) sts. Keeping 5 sts at each end in garter st for front bands, work in k 1, p 1, ribbing for 5 rows.

Next row: Bind off 5 sts, continue in ribbing as established—78 (86) sts.

Following row: Bind off 5 sts, p to end of row; cast on 10 sts at end of row—83 (91) sts.

Next row: K, casting on 10 sts at end of row—93 (101) sts.

HOOD: With wrong side facing, p 11 sts, place marker for casing, work next 71 (79) sts in Row 1 of quilt pat, place second marker for casing, p rem 11 sts. Keeping 11 sts at each end in st st as established on previous row and keeping rem sts in quilt pat as established, work even until 12 rows of quilt pat have been repeated 6 times. Work Rows 1–6 of quilt pat. P next row, dec 1 st over quilt pat st—92 (100) sts.

Following row: K 46 (50) sts. Weave sts from both needles tog to form seam at top of hood. Fold st st casing in half lengthwise toward inside and sew casing along each edge of quilt pat, leaving opening for cord at neck ends of casing.

With 2 strands of yarn, crochet a chain for drawstring to desired length and thread through casing. Make 2 small pom-poms and attach one to each end of drawstring.

FRONT FINISHING: Baste edges of garter st front band together at center Front. With right side of zipper to wrong side on center front opening and beginning zipper at top of garter st band, baste zipper in place. *Larger size only:* Seam edges of Front bands together below zipper. Hand-sew zipper and remove basting threads.

EXPANDING BOTTOM: With right side facing, pick up 67 (75) sts across center of lower edge of Front of bunting. Work in quilt pat for 6 rows, inc 1 st each end on second and fourth rows—71 (79) sts.

Keeping to quilt pat as established, (work 6 rows, inc 1 st each end of second and fourth rows) twice—79 (87) sts.

Continuing in pat as established, (work 6 rows, dec 1 st each end on second and fourth rows) 3 times—67 (75) sts. Bind off.

Sew finished panel in place, easing around sides and back of garter st edge at lower edge of bunting.

For the blanket

With ice blue, cast on 255 sts. Work in garter st (k every row) for 2-inch border, ending with a right side row.

Next row: K 14 sts, place marker for left side border; work Row 1 of quilt pat over center 227 sts, place marker; k 14 sts for right side border. Keeping 14 sts at each edge in ice blue and garter stitch, work quilt pat over center 227 sts in the following color sequence: 23 rows more ice blue ending with Row 12 of quilt pat, 6 rows raspberry, 42 rows pink, 6 rows raspberry; 192 rows ice blue, * 6 rows raspberry, 18 rows pink, 6 rows raspberry, 12 rows ice blue; rep from * 2 times more.

Work all 255 sts in ice blue and garter st for 2 inches; bind off.

Crocheted Peter Pan Collar

Shown on page 136.
Finished size is for child, Size 6.

MATERIALS

DMC Cordonnet Special, Size 20 (174-yard ball): 1 ball white
Size 6 steel crochet hook
1 yard ⅜-inch-wide satin ribbon

Abbreviations: Page 211.

INSTRUCTIONS

Our collar is worked in one piece and begins at the neckline edge. Collar can be worn under an existing collar as shown on page 137, or worn atop a plain neckline edge.

Row 1: Ch 152, sc in second ch from hook, and in each ch across; ch 5, turn.

Note: To work double triple crochet (dtr) in following row, work as follows: Yo hook 3 times and draw up lp in st, (yo, draw through 2 lps on hook) 4 times.

Row 2: Dtr in first st, * ch 1, sk sc, dtr in next 2 sts; rep from * across; ch 1, turn.

Row 3: Sc in each st across; turn. (Rows 2–3 form the heading.)

Row 4: * Ch 11, sk 4 sc, sc in next sc, **ch 4, sc in last sc made, ch 4, sc in same sc, ch 5, drop lp from hook and insert in same sc, pull the dropped ch through—triple picot (trc-picot) made;** repeat from * across; end ch 5, trc in last sc—29 trc-picot made, turn.

Row 5: * Ch 11, sc in center ch of ch-11 lp, work trc-picot; rep from * across; end ch 5, trc in center ch of last lp—28 trc-picot made, turn.

Rows 6–7: Repeat Row 5—26 trc-picot made at end of Row 7.

Row 8: * Ch 10, sc in ch-11 lp; rep from * across; fasten off.

EDGING: *Row 9:* Attach thread at beg of Row 1 and working along ch-10 lp edge, sc in same st as join, 4 sc over post of dtr, * (sc in next st, 4 sc over next lp) 4 times, (10 sc over next ch-10 lp) 26 times; (4 sc in next lp, sc in next st) 4 times, 4 sc around post of dtr, sc in last st, turn.

Row 10: Ch 1, sc in first 10 sc; * turn, ch 4, trc in fifth sc, ch 4, trc in same sc, ch 4, sl st in ninth sc; turn, 3 sc over first ch-4 lp, **ch 3, sc in first ch—picot made;** 2 sc over same lp; 2 sc over next lp, make picot, 2 sc over same lp, sc in next 10 sc, rep from * around collar; fasten off. Thread heading edging with ribbon.

Crocheted Yoke

Shown on page 137.
Finished size is for child, Size 4–5.

MATERIALS
South Maid Mercerized Thread (550-yard ball): 1 ball cream
Size 7 steel crochet hook
1 yard ½-inch-wide satin ribbon

Abbreviations: Page 211.
Gauge: 8 dc = 1 inch; 4 rows = 1 inch.

INSTRUCTIONS
Our yoke piece is hand-sewn to dress when completed. Ribbon is tacked in place at back and woven through the sps of Rnd 2 and tied in bow at front.

Row 1: Ch 116, dc in second ch from hook and in each ch across; ch 2, turn.

Row 2: Dc in next 3 dc, * ch 2, dc in next 3 dc, rep from * across row; end dc in top of turning ch; ch 3, turn.

Row 3: 3 dc in first ch-2 lp, * ch 3, 3 dc in same lp, ch 1, sl st in next ch-2 lp, ch 1, 3 dc in next ch-2 lp; rep from * across; end ch 3, sl st in last dc; turn.

Row 4: Ch 5, sl st in first ch-3 lp, * ch 10, sl st in next ch-3 lp; rep from * across; end ch 5, sl st in top of ch-3; ch 1, turn.

Row 5: 7 sc in first ch-5 lp; in *each* ch-10 lp work 13 sc; 7 sc in last ch-5 lp; ch 3, turn.

Row 6: Trc in first sc, * ch 3, 2 trc in sp bet next 2 sc-grps, ch 1, 2 trc in same sp, ch 3, 2 trc in center sc of next 13 sc-grp, ch 1, 2 trc in same st; rep from * across; end ch 3, 2 trc in last sc; ch 4, turn.

Row 7: Sk first ch-3 lp, * in next ch-1 sp, work trc, ch 1, trc; ch 2, dc in next ch-3 lp, rep from * across; end ch 4, sl st in top of last trc; ch 6, turn.

Row 8: Sk first ch-lp, * 3 dc in next ch-1 sp, ch 4, sk next 2 ch-2 lps; rep from * across; end ch 6, sl st in last st; ch 1, turn.

Row 9: 5 sc in first ch-6 lp, * dc in next dc, ch 2, sk 1 dc, dc in next dc, in next ch-4 lp work 2 dc, ch 2, 2 dc; rep from * across; end dc in next dc, ch 2, sk dc, dc in next dc, 5 sc in last ch-6 lp; turn.

Row 10: Sl st into each of next 2 sc, * in next ch-2 lp work 3 dc, ch 3, 3 dc; sc in next ch-2 lp; rep from * across; end sc in third sc; ch 5, turn.

Row 11: Sl st in ch-3 lp, * ch 9, sl st in next ch-3 lp; rep from * across; end ch 5, sl st in next st; ch 1, turn.

Row 12: 5 sc in ch-5 lp, 11 sc in *each* ch-9 lp; end 5 sc in last ch-5 lp; ch 3, turn.

Row 13: 2 dc in sp bet next 2 sc-grps, * ch 2, in center sc of next 11 sc-grp work 2 dc, ch 1, 2 dc; ch 2, trc in sp bet next 2 sc-grps; rep from * across; end ch 2, 2 dc in sp between last 2 sc-grps, ch 3, sl st in last st; ch 1, turn.

Row 14: 3 sc in first ch-3 lp, * sc in ch-1 lp, 3 sc in next ch-3 lp; rep from * across; end 3 sc in last lp; fasten off. Weave ribbon through ch-2 sps of Rnd 2.

Crocheted Sailor Collar

Shown on pages 136–137.
Finished size is for Child, Size 4–5.

MATERIALS
J. & P. Coats Knit-Cro-Sheen (400- yard ball): 1 ball cream
Size 7 steel crochet hook
2 purchased appliqués

Abbreviations: Page 211.
Gauge: 10 sts = 1 inch; 10 rows = 1 inch.

INSTRUCTIONS
COLLAR BACK: Pattern st is reversible. Beg at lower back edge of collar, ch 110.

Row 1: Sc in second from hook, and in each ch across—109 sc; ch 1, turn.

Row 2: Sc in *front* lp of first st, * sc in *back* lp of next sc, sc in *front* lp of next st; rep from * across row; ch 1, turn.

Rep Row 2 for pat for 3½ inches.

Note: Sc in the front loop falls over a sc in the front loop of the previous row.

SHOULDER AND NECK SHAPINGS: Inc 1 st each side every 4 rows 11 times and *at same time* when piece measures 4½ inches, divide work for neck edge and work along 1 side of collar as follows: Work across 44 sts in pat, turn.

Keeping to pat and continuing to inc at shoulder edge, dec 1 st at neck edge every row 15 times, every other row 6 times, every fourth row 2 times, every other row until 2 sts rem; work 1 row even; fasten off.

Attach thread 44 sts in from rem shoulder edge, and work neck and shoulder shapings to correspond with first side.

EDGING: Attach thread in first st along outside edge of collar, ch 1, * sk 2 sts, 5 dc in next st, sk 2 sts, sl st in next st; rep from * around to opposite edge of collar; fasten off. Tack appliqués to corners on back of collar.

Knitted Sheep Pullover Sweater

Shown on page 138.
Directions are for Size 2; changes for Sizes 4, 6, 8, 10, 12, and 14 follow in parentheses. Finished chest = 22¼ (24¼, 26¼, 28¼, 30¼, 32¼, 34¼) inches.

MATERIALS

Brunswick Pomfret Sport Yarn (50-gram balls): 4 (4, 6, 8, 8, 10, 12) balls of No. 501 periwinkle blue or No. 5151 calypso pink (MC), and 2 (2, 2, 3, 3, 4, 4) balls No. 500 white (CC)
Sizes 2 and 5 standard knitting needles, or size to obtain gauge given below
Sizes 2 and 5 circular needles in the following lengths: *For Sizes 2 and 4:* 16 inches long; *For Sizes 6 and 8:* 22 inches long; *For Sizes 10, 12, and 14:* 24 inches long
2 stitch markers

Abbreviations: Page 217.
Gauge: With larger needles over st st, 6 sts = 1 inch; 8 rows = 1 inch.

INSTRUCTIONS

Note on 2-color knitting: When changing yarn colors always twist the new color around the color in use to prevent making holes. Carry unused yarn loosely across the back of work, twisting it around the yarn in use every 3 or 4 stitches.

BODY: Garment is worked in 1 piece to underarm. With smaller circular needle and MC, cast on 124 (136, 148, 160, 172, 184, 196) sts; join, being careful not to twist sts. Work k 1, p 1 ribbing over 62 (68, 74, 80, 86, 92, 98) sts for Front, place marker A to indicate side seam; work k 1, p 1 ribbing to end of rnd for Back, place marker B. (*Note:* Sl markers each rnd.) Continue in rib as established for 2 (2, 2, 2, 2½, 2½, 2½) inches.

Rnd 1: Change to circular needle and st st, inc 10 sts evenly spaced—134 (146, 158, 170, 182, 194, 206) sts around; 67 (73, 79, 85, 91, 97, 103) sts across Front and Back.

Rnd 2: Work even.

Rnd 3: Establish fleck pat as follows: * Beg Chart 1 at C (D, A, B, C, A, B) and work to T 3 (3, 4, 4, 4, 5, 5) times; then work from T to X (Z, W, Y, Z, V, W) once. Sl marker A and rep from * across the Back; sl marker B.

Rnd 4: Work even.

Rnd 5: Work from chart as established in Rnd 3 and rep Chart 1 through Rnd 18.

Continue working fleck pat as established, working pat in every fourth row and staggering fleck in every fourth st as in Rnds 19–23 until total length measures 7 (8, 9, 10, 11½, 12½, 13½) inches or desired length to underarm, ending 3 (4, 4, 5, 5, 6, 6) sts before end of last rnd.

ARMHOLE SHAPING: (*Note:* Front and Back are worked separately from this point.) Keeping to fleck pat, bind off next 6 (8, 8, 10, 10, 12, 12) sts; work 61 (65, 71, 75, 81, 85, 91) sts for Front and sl to holder; bind off 6 (8, 8, 10, 10, 12, 12) sts for rem armhole; work rem 61 (65, 71, 75, 81, 85, 91) sts for Back. Continue on these sts back and forth in rows with standard needles, dec 1 st each end every other row 3 (4, 5, 6, 7, 8, 9) times)—55 (57, 61, 63, 67, 69, 73) sts.

Work even, keeping to fleck pat until length past beg of armholes measures 4 (4½, 5, 5½, 6, 6½, 7) inches, ending with a wrong-side row.

NECK SHAPING: Work 22 (22, 22, 21, 22, 22, 23) sts; join second ball of yarn and bind off center 11 (13, 17, 21, 23, 25, 27) sts; complete row. Working both sides at the same time and keeping to fleck pat, bind off at neck edge every other row 3 sts, then bind off 2 sts—17 (17, 17, 16, 17, 17, 18) sts each side.

SHOULDER: Work even until length past beg of armholes measures 4½ (5, 5½, 6, 6½, 7, 7½) inches. Bind off rem sts.

FRONT: Work same as for Back until length past beg of armholes measures 2½ (3, 3¼, 3½, 4, 4, 4½) inches, ending with a wrong-side row.

NECK SHAPING: Work 22 (22, 22, 21, 22, 22, 23) sts; join second ball of yarn and bind off center 11 (13, 17, 21, 23, 25, 27) sts; complete row. Working both sides at the same time, bind off at neck edge every other row 3 sts, then bind off 2 sts—17 (17, 17, 16, 17, 17, 18) sts rem each side. Work even until length past beg of armholes measures 4½ (5, 5½, 6, 6½, 7, 7½) inches. Bind off rem sts.

SLEEVES: With smaller standard needles and MC cast on 40 (42, 44, 48, 50, 53, 55) sts. Work k 1, p 1 ribbing for 2 (2, 2, 2½, 2½, 2½, 2½) inches.

Row 1: Change to larger needles and st st, inc 4 sts evenly spaced across row—44 (46, 48, 52, 54, 57, 59) sts.

Row 2 and all even-numbered rows: P.

Row 3: Establish fleck pat as follows: Beg Chart 2 at A (B, B, D, D, E, F) and work to T 2 times; then work form T to V (V, W, W, X, Y, Y) to complete row.

Row 4: Work even.

Row 5: Work from chart as established in Row 3 and rep chart through Row 19.

Continue to work in fleck pat as established working pat in every fourth row and staggering fleck in every fourth st.

At the same time, beg with Row 7, inc 1 st at each end every 1 inch 4 (4, 5, 5, 6, 6, 8) times, working inc sts in Chart 2 pat—52 (54, 58, 62, 66, 69, 75) sts. Work even until total length of sleeve measures 9 (10, 11, 12, 13½, 14½, 15½) inches, or desired length to underarm, ending with a wrong-side row.

TOP SHAPING: Keeping to pat, bind off 3 (4, 4, 5, 5, 6, 6) sts at beg of next 2 rows. Dec 1 st each end every other row 11 (12, 13, 14, 16, 16, 18) times—24 (22, 24, 24, 24, 25, 27) sts. Bind off 3 sts at beg of next 4 rows—12 (10, 12, 12, 12, 13, 15) sts. Bind off rem sts.

FINISHING: Sew shoulder seams. Sew sleeve seams and set in sleeves.

NECKBAND: With smaller circular needle and MC, pick up and k 96 (98, 100, 102, 106, 108, 110) sts evenly around neck edge. Work k 1, p 1 ribbing for 1½ (1½, 1½, 1½, 2, 2, 2) inches. Without binding off, fold ribbing to inside and sew in place stitch by stitch.

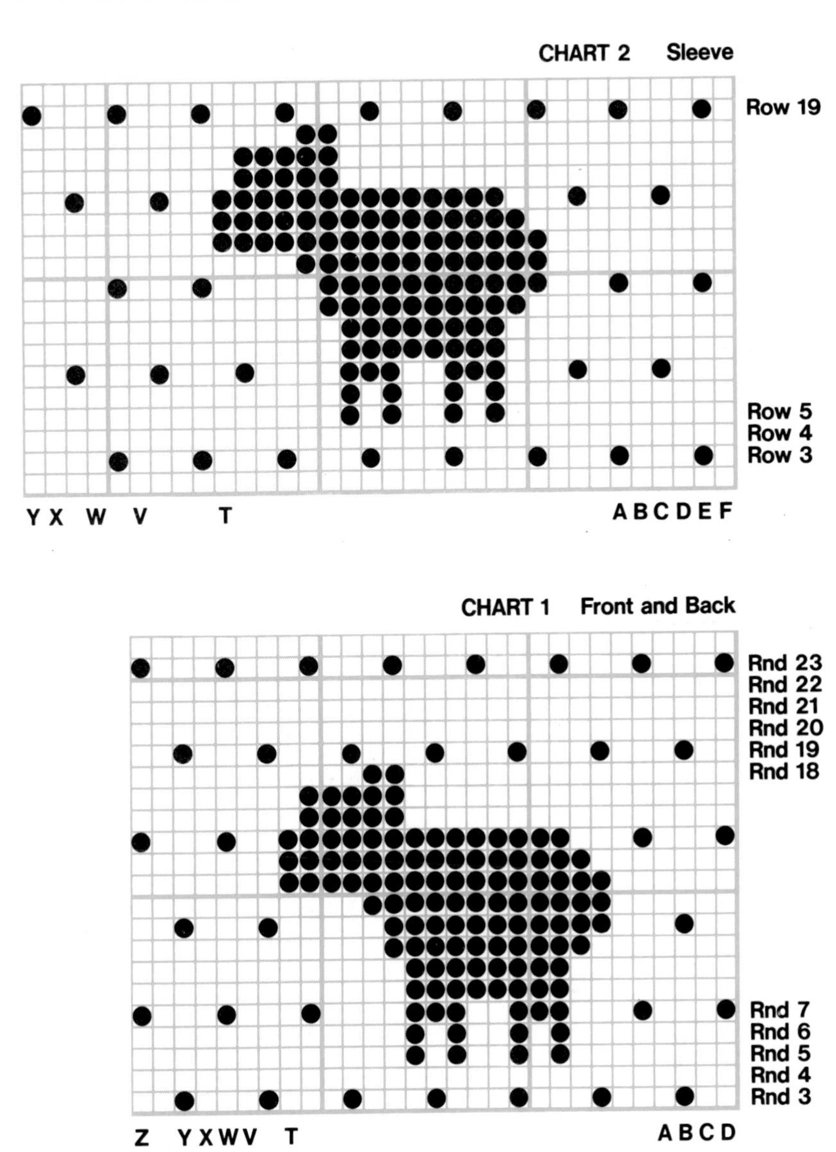

Make Your Youngster's Sweaters Special

Kids love to wear clothing embellished with favorite motifs—hearts, ducks, or rocket ships, for example. Using the how-to instructions for the sheep sweater, *above,* you can personalize any child's garment.

Begin by drawing an outline (actual size) of the motif onto a piece of paper. Then, work a swatch of knitting in stockinette stitch using the yarns and needles you intend to use for the project. Measure your gauge. From your yarn shop you can purchase knitting grid paper that will approximate the gauge of your knitted swatch.

Trace your drawing onto the grid paper to make a pattern for your knitting. Determine the width *in stitches* of the motif, allow a few stitches for spacing between motifs, and arrange the design in a balanced sequence across the sweater front, back, and sleeves.

Knitted Seaside Vest Sweater

Shown on page 139.
Directions are for Size 2; changes for Sizes 4, 6, 8, 10, 12, and 14 follow in parentheses. Finished chest = 22 (24, 26½, 29, 21, 33½, 34½) inches.

MATERIALS

Tahki Cotton Twist (100-gram skeins): 2 (2, 2, 2, 2, 3, 4) skeins of No. 779 blue (color A); 1 skein *each* of No. 771 white (color B) and No. 772 ecru (color C)

Sizes 6 and 7 knitting needles, or size to obtain gauge given below

Size 6 double-pointed needles

Abbreviations: Page 217.

Gauge: With larger needles over st st, 5 sts = 1 inch; 13 rows = 2 inches.

INSTRUCTIONS

Note on 2-color knitting: When changing yarn colors always twist the new color around the color in use to prevent making holes. Carry unused yarn loosely across the back of work, twisting it around the yarn in use every 3 or 4 stitches.

FRONT: With smaller needles and A, cast on 57 (63, 69, 75, 81, 87, 89) sts. Work in k 1, p 1 ribbing for 1½ inches. Change to larger needles, color C and st st (k right side row, p wrong side row), and work from chart, *right,* for 62 (64, 66, 70, 74, 78, 80) rows.

ARMHOLE AND SHOULDER SHAPING: Bind off 4 sts at beg of next 2 rows, then dec 1 st each end every other row 3 (3, 3, 4, 4, 4, 4) times—43 (49, 55, 59, 65, 71, 73) sts. When 16 (18, 20, 22, 24, 26, 28) rows past beg of armhole shaping have been completed, k 15 (17, 19, 21, 23, 25, 26) and sl to holder for left shoulder. Bind off center 13 (15, 17, 17, 19, 21, 21) sts; complete row. On right shoulder, work to neck.

Next row: Dec 1 st at neck edge every other row 5 (7, 7, 7, 7, 7, 7) times—10 (10, 12, 14, 16, 18, 19) sts. As chart is finished, sl rem sts to holder for shoulder.

Join yarn to left shoulder and finish as for right shoulder, reversing shapings.

BACK: With smaller needles and A, cast on 57 (63, 69, 75, 81, 87, 89) sts and work k 1, p 1 ribbing for 1½ inches. Change larger needles and st st and work even until length to armhole shaping equals that of Front, ending with a wrong-side row. Bind off 4 sts at beg of next 2 rows, then dec 1 st each end every other row 3 (3, 3, 4, 4, 4, 4) times. Work even until length to shoulder equals that of Front. Sl all sts to holder.

FINISHING: Weave or k shoulder sts tog. Sew side seams.

NECKBAND: With right side facing, using double-pointed needles, and A, pick up 84 (88, 92, 96, 100, 104, 108) sts around neck edge and work k 1, p 1 ribbing for 5 rows. Bind off in ribbing.

ARMHOLE BANDS: With right side facing, using double-pointed needles and A, pick up 60 (62, 64, 66, 68, 70, 72) sts around armhole edge and work k 1, p 1 ribbing for 5 rows. Bind off in ribbing.

Knitting with Bobbins

When you are knitting in rows, use bobbins to simplify changing colors; you'll no longer have to carry an entire ball of yarn for every color in the design. Here are some tips to help you use bobbins.

Bobbins generally are available in two sizes. Use the smaller size for baby, fingering, sock, and other light-weight yarns. Use the larger size for sport, worsted, or bulky-weight yarns.

To determine how much yarn you need on a bobbin, estimate the width of the area to be stitched in a color. Cut yarn for the bobbin four times longer than your estimate.

Use a separate bobbin for each color, except the main color, in the design you are stitching.

To fill the bobbin, wrap yarn *horizontally* around the bobbin three times; then wrap it *vertically* once to fasten it in the slot. Continue wrapping until you've wound all the yarn or the bobbin is full.

Avoid overloading the bobbin. It is better to wind and tie in another bobbin at a convenient point in your work than to wrap it too tightly or too full. Join a new bobbin where colors change or wherever joining will not be obvious.

As you stitch across a row and come to a new color, drop the color in use on the side the stitch ends (knits at back of work, purls at front). With the right hand, pick up the new color from *beneath* the old one; work the next stitch. Bringing the new yarn *under* the old yarn twists the yarns together and makes a loop that prevents a hole from forming where the two colors join.

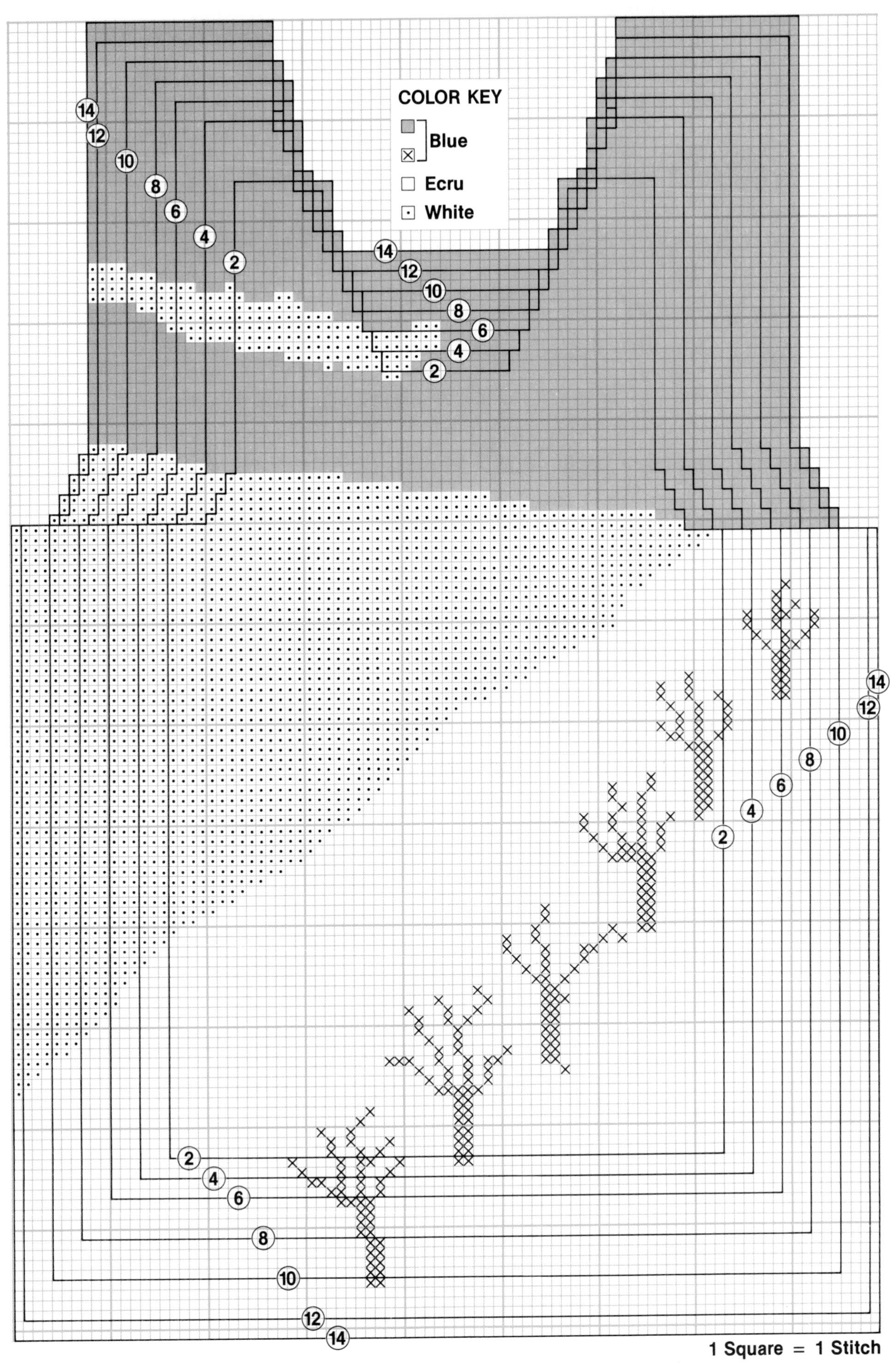

1 Square = 1 Stitch

New Projects From Old Favorites

Certain patterns are too pretty—and too versatile—to be used only once. By changing the materials you work with, using just a portion of a favorite design, or adapting instructions from one project to a different one, you'll be able to stitch your favorite patterns again and again into home and fashion accessories and gifts for family and friends.

A perfect example of the "one pattern, many projects" plan is the graceful oval design used for the crocheted place mat and rug pictured here.

Worked in cotton thread with a small steel hook, this pattern yields lovely ovals for a country-style table setting. If you follow the same pattern using ¾-inch-wide strips of fabric and a hefty, Size K crochet hook, you'll soon have a charming scatter rug that can be worked to any size, and in any color combination you desire.

Adorning a decorative straw hat, *far right,* are more old favorites—a garland of colorful crocheted flowers similar to those shown on page 113.

For instructions for the place mat, rug, and hat, see page 206.

NEW PROJECTS FROM OLD FAVORITES

If you discover a sweater pattern that fits particularly well, or one that has features you're especially fond of, it's more than likely that the design will turn up in several different colors in your closet.

But there are other, more imaginative ways to put a favorite sweater pattern to use. Here, for example, we picked up the sleeves from a much-loved knitted cardigan, *near right,* and substituted them for the fabric sleeves on a simple wool jacket design, *far right.* The result is a new, designer-look garment with all the comfortable feel and sure fit of your favorite old clothes.

Instructions begin on page 207.

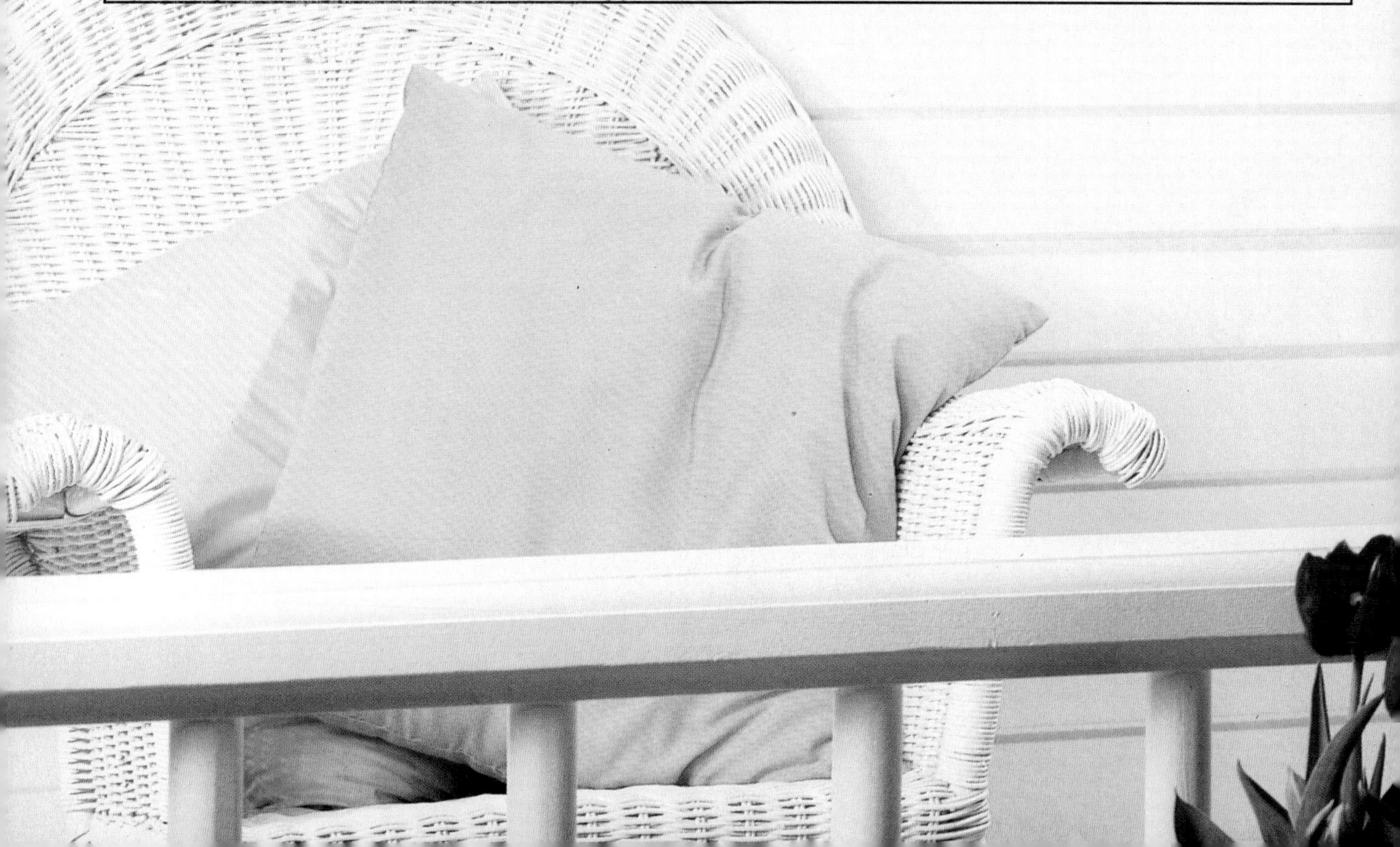

NEW PROJECTS FROM OLD FAVORITES

Having once mastered the intricacies of Fair Isle and fisherman-style knitting, you'll enjoy the challenge of working these designs into all sorts of different projects. The richly patterned afghan pictured at *far right* combines samples of these two types of knitted patterns to spectacular effect.

Motifs for the center panel of this 42x57-inch afghan are lifted directly from a sweater vest pattern, *above right,* and the two side panels repeat designs used on the sleeves of an elegant fisherman-knit sweater, *below right.*

If you're not quite ready to tackle such an ambitious project, you might stitch just one or two bands of a favorite Fair Isle pattern into the border of an afghan worked in stockinette or garter stitch. Or customize a classic sweater with a band of motifs worked just above the ribbing.

Instructions for the afghan begin on page 207.

The Loveliness of Lace

ROMANTIC ACCENTS FOR EVERY ROOM

The charm and grace of a bygone era inspired this collection of lacy accessories for your home. Dainty floral designs, lavish crocheted edgings, and intricately patterned doilies are touches that bespeak a romantic vision, whatever the setting.

Summer roses are preserved forever in delicate panels of filet crochet on the patchwork coverlet and pillow pictured here. The coverlet measures 56x60 inches. If you wish to alter the size, simply vary the number of blocks or the width of the fabric strips used to frame each crocheted panel.

A graceful variation of the leaf and bud pattern from the panel border was adapted for the ruffle on the pillow. For a coordinated look, you might use this same edging as a border for curtains, a tablecloth, or even a dust ruffle. Directions begin on page 168.

ROMANTIC ACCENTS

Floral designs of every description are among the most popular of all crochet motifs.

The open rose on the richly textured afghan at *right* is a variation of a floral design adapted from an old-fashioned thread doily dating from the mid-1930s. And the graceful arrangement of hexagons is reminiscent of the traditional Grandmother's Flower Garden quilt pattern—a perennial favorite with patchwork enthusiasts for more than a century.

The three-dimensional blossoms on this afghan are worked in a modified version of traditional Irish crochet techniques. Yellow-centered rosettes and accent leaves are stitched in springlike shades of sport yarn—azalea pink, soft heather, deep amethyst, and jade green. Center blossoms are framed with six white petals to complete each motif.

You may wish to change the color scheme to suit your own decor. Or, instead of limiting your selection of colors, you might use scraps of sport yarn in a collection of floral colors for the rosettes and choose several shades of green for the leaves. Scatter the colors at random across the surface of the afghan, just as Mother Nature does in the garden. It's an excellent opportunity to use leftover scraps of yarn.

A total of 67 hexagons are joined to make this 53-inch-square throw. A fringe of plump, six-inch-long tassels adds to the luxurious effect.

To make a spread-size afghan, simply increase the number of motif blocks. For a smaller project, stitch together seven hexagonal motifs (one in the center, surrounded by six more blossoms) for a country-fresh, pillow-top doily.

For an altogether different look, try working the pattern in fine white or ecru cotton thread, using a smaller crochet hook. The result is a light and lacy throw that might be just right for draping atop a small table or across the family piano. It can even do double duty as a summer stole.

Keep in mind that most crochet motifs, particularly block designs, change their character depending on the materials used. Many motifs are suitable for more than one purpose—from afghans to clothing inserts or appliqués. Their use is limited only by your skills and imagination.

To kindle your creative energies, experiment with threads and yarns of different weights, using hooks in various sizes.

Keep the samples in your workbasket, along with notes on those you like best, projects for which the sample threads and patterns might be suitable, and other ideas that occur to you as you stitch. To get started, see the "Creative Stitching" sections of this book.

ROMANTIC ACCENTS FOR EVERY ROOM

Elegant handmade doilies were the grace notes in many Victorian parlors. These ornamental scraps of needleart served to protect the highly polished furniture, cushion a beloved bit of bric-a-brac, and, just coincidentally, display the handiwork of the mistress of the house.

Today, we treasure these mementos of an earlier day when fine needlework was highly prized and diligently practiced by ladies young and old, of every rank and station. Few of us have the time or the inclination to create these dainty coverings for every exposed surface in our modern-day parlors. But an exquisite doily or two can still bring a welcome romantic flourish to many contemporary settings.

The intricately patterned knitted doily, *above right,* is a treasured antique, grand enough to be the prize in any needlework collection. Measuring a generous 15½ inches in diameter, the doily is stitched in gossamer threads using the finest double-pointed needles. Only the most experienced knitters will want to attempt to execute a copy—but for those who do, the result is sure to be worth the effort.

Because tension varies from knitter to knitter, your finished doily may vary in size from the original. Using slightly larger needles and a coarser cotton thread, you can make a delightful round tablecloth with the same pattern.

Elegant when used alone, this outsize doily also is lovely displayed over a cloth in a contrasting color. Or, work the same pattern in concentric rounds of different colored threads for yet another effect.

Each of the crocheted doilies, *opposite,* features a variation of the popular pineapple motif.

The Flower Ring doily, *bottom left,* features a circlet of nine tiny flowers in its center. Graceful scallops border a second doily, *above left,* and a ring of *fleurs-de-lis* surrounds the center on the third doily, *center right.*

Knitted doilies tend to be too stretchy for appliqué, but slightly heavier crocheted doilies, such as those shown here, are ideal for appliqué and make delightful pillow fronts.

When appliquéing any doily to a purchased or made-to-order pillow front, first pin and baste the doily in place to prevent shifting. Then, working in circles from the center of the lace outward, carefully tack the doily to the ground fabric at regular intervals.

Use tiny, invisible stitches and sewing thread in a matching color. Once the doily has been stitched into place, remove the basting threads and gently press.

ROMANTIC ACCENTS

For generations, filet crochet has been the delight of both lace collectors and talented crafters. One reason for its continuing popularity is its simplicity. The characteristic geometric patterns, formed by tiny clusters of stitches on an airy mesh background, look intricate, but they're actually quite easy to create.

Classic filet crochet edgings include a heart motif on the tablecloth, *opposite and below,* a rose design on the middle cloth, and a scallop pattern worked in a heavier thread on the bottom cloth.

A cozy cottage scene is stitched into the antimacassar shown on the chair. A simple star pattern doily makes the pillow top. If you're a novice at filet work, the star pattern is an ideal first project.

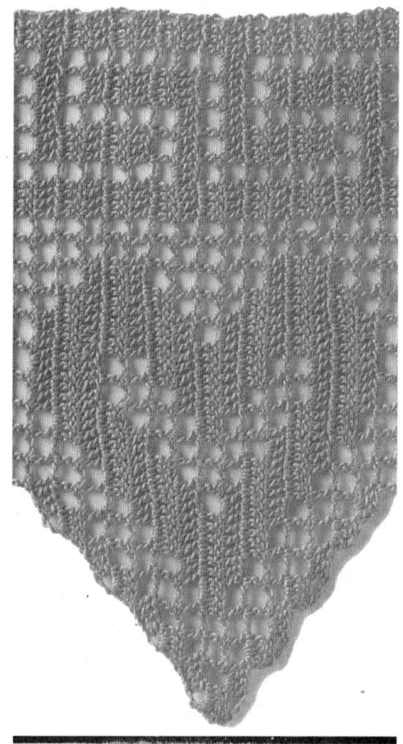

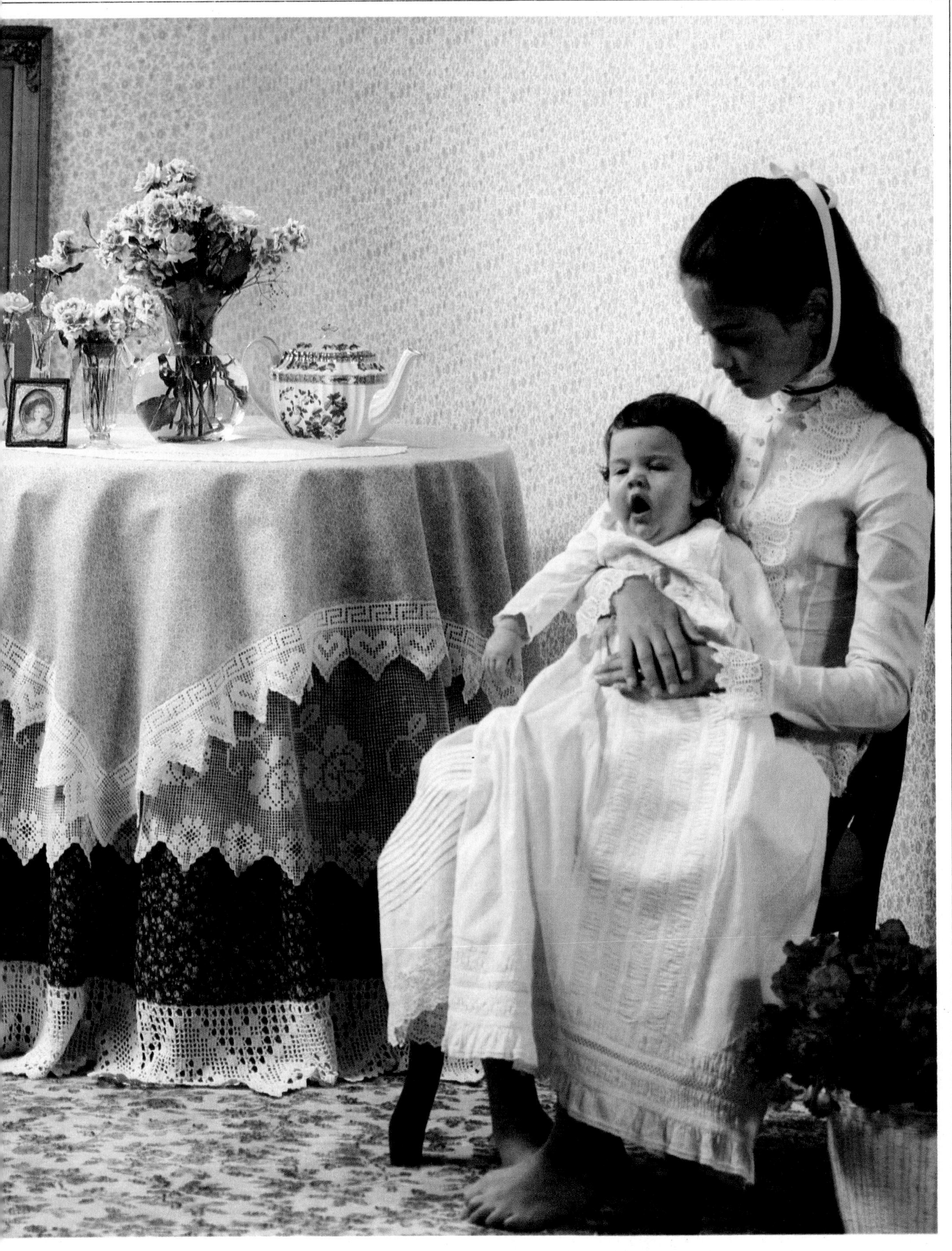

Filet Crochet Rose Coverlet and Pillow

Shown on pages 162–163.
Finished size of coverlet is 56x60 inches, excluding the ruffle. One crocheted block measures 15x16 inches. Edging measures 5¼ inches wide.

MATERIALS

For the crochet blocks and edging

DMC Cébélia Crochet Cotton (563-yard balls): 6 balls of white, Size 30
Size 14 steel crochet hook

For the quilt

1½ yards of burgundy pindot fabric for backing behind crochet blocks
½ yard of 2 dark fabric prints for inside border strips
½ yard of 2 light fabric prints for inside border strips
⅔ yard of 2 dark fabric prints for outside border strips
⅔ yard of 2 light fabric prints for outside border strips
Scraps of prints or plaids for squares
1⅔ yards of 60-inch-wide or 3½ yards of 44-inch-wide printed fabric for backing
Quilt batting and thread

For the pillow

½ yard of burgundy pindot fabric for backing behind crocheted block
1 yard print fabric for pillow backing and ruffle
Polyester fiberfill
2⅝ yards cotton cording to make piping
Contrasting fabric to cover cotton cording

Abbreviations: Page 211.
Gauge: 15 dc = 1 inch; 7 rows dc = 1 inch.

INSTRUCTIONS

For the filet square

Ch 303. *Row 1:* Dc in fourth ch from hook and in each ch across—301 dc, counting beg ch-3 as first dc; ch 3, turn. (*Note:* 301 dc is equivalent to 100 blocks.)

Row 2: **Dc in each of next 3 dc—beg block (bl) over bl made; * ch 2, sk 2 dc, dc in next dc—space (sp) over bl made.** Rep from * to last 3 sts, ending with **dc in each of last 2 dc and top of ch-3—end bl over bl made;** ch 3, turn.

Row 3: Work beg bl over bl; **ch 2, sk ch-2 sp, dc in next dc—sp over sp made;** make 4 more sps; **2 dc in next sp, dc in next dc—bl over sp made;** then work 10 sps, 1 bl, 14 sps, 3 bls, 6 sps, 1 bl, 18 sps, 5 bls, 5 sps, 5 bls, 2 sps, 1 bl, 1 sp, 1 bl, 2 sps, 1 bl, 8 sps, 1 bl, 7 sps, end bl over bl; ch 3, turn.

Beg with Row 4 of chart, *opposite,* work as established, reading even-numbered rows from left to right and odd-numbered rows from right to left. Make 4 squares for quilt, 1 for pillow. Block squares.

For the edging

For quilt edging, work 18 repeats for top edge. For pillow, work 21 repeats; whipstitch ends together.

Beg at side edge, ch 77.

Row 1: Dc in eighth ch from hook; **ch 2, sk 2 ch, dc in next ch—sp made;** dc in each of next 3 ch; (ch 2, sk 2 ch, dc in next ch) 12 times—12 sps made; dc in next 3 ch, 2 sps over next 6 ch, dc in next 3 ch; 3 sps over next 9 ch, dc in rem 6 ch; ch 3, turn.

Row 2: **Dc in next 6 dc—2 bls over 2 bls made; ch 2, sk ch-2 sp, dc in next dc—sp over sp made;** work 2 more sp over sp; **ch 2, sk 2 dc, dc in next dc—sp over bl made;** work 2 more sp over sp, dc in next 3 dc, work 11 sp over sp, **2 dc in ch-2 sp, dc in next dc—bl over sp made;** work sp over bl, sp over sp; do not work in last sp—dec made at end of row; turn.

Row 3: **Sl st in next 2 ch and dc—dec made at beg of row; ch 5, sk ch-2 sp, dc in next dc—beg sp made;** sp over bl, bl over sp, (sp over sp) 10 times, bl over bl, bl over sp, (sp over sp) 5 times, 2 bls over 2 bls; ch 3, turn.

Beg with Row 4 of chart, *below,* work Rows 4–7. Work even-numbered rows from left to right, odd-numbered rows from right to left.

Row 8: Work 2 bls, 4 sps, 3 bls, 8 sps, 1 bl, 1 sp; **wrap thread over hook 3 times, draw up lp in same st as last dc, (yo, and draw**

FILET EDGING

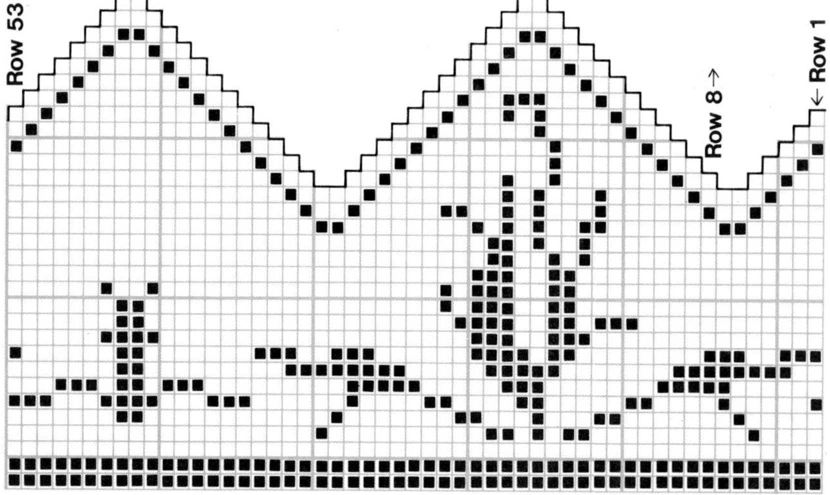

□ Space (sp) ■ Block (bl)

through 2 lps on hook) 4 times—sp inc at end of row; ch 7, turn.

Row 9: **Dc in first dc (last dc of previous row)—sp inc at beg of row;** complete row; ch 3, turn.

Follow chart for Rows 10–53 working sp increases and decreases at beginning of rows as established; then rep Rows 2–53 for pat until edging is desired length, or for required number of motifs, ending with Row 52 of pat; fasten off.

Quilt assembly: *Note:* Finished size of each quilt block is 28x27 inches.

All sewing directions and measurements allow for ¼-inch seam allowances.

Cut four burgundy pieces, *each* 15½x16½ inches. For the *inside* border strips, cut four dark and four light strips, *each* 15½x3½ inches; also cut four dark and four light strips, *each* 16½x3½ inches.

For the *outside* border strips, cut four dark and four light strips, *each* 21½x3½ inches; cut four dark and four light strips, *each* 22½x3½ inches.

Cut 32 squares from scrap fabrics, each 3½x3½ inches.

Using the photograph as a guide, sew one dark and one light 15½-inch strip to the 15½-inch sides of the burgundy blocks.

continued

FILET SQUARE

Assemble the other two side strips by sewing two squares to both ends of the 16½-inch strips. Center and sew these strips to the 16½-inch sides of the burgundy blocks and the first border strips.

Sew one dark and one light 21½-inch strip to the two short ends of the pieced block. Assemble the remaining side strips by joining two small squares to both ends of the 22½-inch strips and sew these strips to the other two sides to complete the blocks.

Sew the crocheted pieces atop the burgundy pindot blocks. With right sides together, stitch the four blocks together.

Piece and cut the backing fabric to measure 3 inches beyond the outside edges of the assembled top. Layer the backing (wrong side up), batting, and top (right side up); baste all layers together. Machine- or hand-quilt along the seam edges of the border strips and the 3-inch squares.

Fold backing fabric to make a 1-inch-wide border on each side of the quilt. Turn under raw edges; trim away excess backing and batting. Blindstitch backing into place on front; remove basting threads. Gather edging slightly; hand-sew to one short edge of coverlet.

Pillow assembly

Note: All sewing directions and cutting measurements allow for ½-inch seam allowances.

Cut two 16x17-inch blocks, one from burgundy pindot fabric and one from backing fabric.

For the fabric ruffle, cut three 11x36-inch strips. Stitch the short ends together to make a circular strip. Fold strip in half, lengthwise, with wrong sides together and raw edges even. Sew a gathering thread on the seam line; set aside.

Cover the cotton cording with the contrasting fabric; set aside.

Center and stitch the crocheted block to the burgundy block. With right sides facing, baste the piping, then the crocheted edging (slightly gathered) to the pillow top. Gather the fabric ruffle to fit the pillow top and baste into place.

Sew backing block to pillow top, right sides together; leave an opening for turning. (Pin the ruffles to the pillow top to avoid catching them in the seams.) Clip seams, turn, stuff, and sew opening closed.

Crocheted Floral Afghan

Shown on pages 162–163.
Finished size is 53x53 inches, excluding fringe.

MATERIALS

Brunswick Pomfret yarn (50-gram balls): 22 balls of No. 500 white (includes 2 balls for fringe); 9 balls *each* of No. 5022 azalea and No. 515 pink heather; 6 balls No. 597 amethyst; 2 balls *each* of No. 567 jade green, No. 580 scotch heather, and No. 503 light yellow

Size G crochet hook

Abbreviations: Page 211.

Gauge: Each motif measures 8 inches from point to point.

INSTRUCTIONS

Make 67 motifs, 25 with azalea petals and jade green leaves, 27 with pink heather petals and scotch heather leaves, and 15 with amethyst petals and scotch heather leaves. Begin motifs with yellow; work petals, then leaves, and finish hexagon with white. Flower colors are scattered randomly in the afghan. Refer to chart, *opposite,* for color sequencing as you work. Join motifs together on the ninth round.

FIRST STRIP (make 7 motifs): With yellow, ch 5; join with sl st to form ring.

Rnd 1: Work 12 sc in ring; join with sl st to first sc. Fasten off.

Rnd 2: Join yarn for flower in any sc, ch 1, sc in same st as joining, * ch 2, sk sc, sc in next sc; rep from * around; join last ch-2 with sl st to first sc—6 ch-2 lps made.

Rnd 3: Ch 1, sc in same st as join; * in next ch-2 lp work (sc, hdc, 3 dc, hdc, sc), sc in next sc; rep from * around; ending sc in sc at beg of rnd. *Rnd 4:* * Ch 2, in same st work (3 dc, ch 2, sc, ch 2, 3 dc, ch 2, sc); ch 5, sc in sc bet next 2 petals; rep from * around; join last ch-5 with sl st to first sc.

Rnd 5: * Ch 1, holding petals of Rnd 4 forward, in next ch-5 lp work **(sc, hdc, 3 dc, sc, 3 dc, hdc, sc—double petal made);** rep from * around; end ch 1, join with sl st in ch-1 sp at beg of rnd—6 double petal-grps made; fasten off.

Rnd 6: Attach green in any ch-1 sp bet 2 double petal-grps. **Ch 3, trc in same sp, ch 1, sl st in trc just made, ch 3, sl st in same sp—leaf made.** * (Ch 3, sk 3 sts, sl st from *back* around post of next dc, ch 4, sl st from *back* around post of center dc of next petal, ch 3, sc in ch-1 sp bet next 2 double petal-groups) twice; make leaf in same ch-1 sp; rep from * once; rep between ( )s twice, join to first ch of beg ch-3—3 leaves made; fasten off.

Rnd 7: Attach white in any ch-4 lp, ch 3, in same lp work (2 dc, ch 2, 3 dc); * (ch 2, sc in next ch-3 lp) twice; ch 2, in next ch-4 lp work 3 dc, ch 2, 3 dc; rep from the * around, holding leaves forward as you work; end with ch 2, join to ch-3 at beg of rnd.

Rnd 8: Ch 3, dc in next 2 dc; * in ch-2 sp work (3 dc, ch 2, 3 dc), dc in next 3 dc; ch 2, sk next ch-2 lp, sc in next ch-2 lp, ch 2, dc in next 3 dc; rep from * around; end with ch-2, join to top of ch-3 at beg of rnd.

Rnd 9: Ch 3, dc in next 3 dc; *** ch 3, sl st in last dc made—picot lp made;** dc in next 2 dc; in ch-2 sp work (3 dc, picot lp, 3 dc); dc in next 2 dc, make picot lp; dc in next 4 dc, ch 4, sl st in third ch from hook, ch 1, sk next 2 ch-2 lps, dc in next 4 dc; rep from * around; join last ch-1 to top of ch-3; fasten off.

Work second motif same as first motif through Rnd 8. Then work through Rnd 9 until ready to begin the fourth point.

Join motifs as follows: In ch-2 sp of fourth point work 3 dc, ch 1, drop hook from work, insert hook in picot lp of point of first motif and draw the dropped lp through, ch 1, work 3 dc in same ch-2 sp of motif in progress, dc in next 2 dc, ch 1, drop hook from work, insert hook in corresponding picot lp of first motif, draw the dropped lp through, ch 1, (dc in next 4 dc of motif in progress, ch 1, drop hook from work, insert hook in corresponding picot of first motif, draw dropped lp through, ch 1) twice; dc in next 2 dc of motif in progress, in ch-2 sp work 3 dc, ch 1, join to picot of first motif, work rem motif as established in Rnd 9 with no more joinings; fasten off.

Complete first strip (7 motifs), working flowers according to chart and joining hexagons as directed for the second motif.

SECOND STRIP (8 motifs): Work through Rnd 8 of first motif; proceed with joinings as established for Rnd 9 in the second motif, *except* work joinings in lower right side of first motif of the first strip.

SECOND MOTIF, SECOND STRIP: Begin joinings in second point of this motif; work joinings in 13 picot lps. Begin joinings in the second motif of the first strip, continue joinings in first motif of first strip and to first motif of second strip. Complete motif as established in pat with no more joinings.

Work rem motifs in this strip as established for this motif.

THIRD STRIP, FIRST MOTIF: Work as for second motif of second strip, *except* there will be joinings in 9 picot lps instead of 13 lps.

Continue to work as established for second motif of second strip to complete rem strips. There will be 5 strips with 7 motifs and 4 strips with 8 motifs.

FRINGE: Cut white yarn into 520 twelve-inch lengths. With bundles of 10 strands, make tassel fringe in space between joinings of motifs and spaces between the 2 motifs on either side of joinings. There will be 26 tassels on each of the afghan ends.

Knitted Lace Doily

Shown on page 164.

Note: This project is recommended for experienced knitters only. Finished size is approximately 15½ inches in diameter. Needles indicated in the materials list are the smallest size available. Because knitting tension varies with knitters, the finished doily may be different than the size noted above.

MATERIALS

Clark's Big Ball 3-Cord Mercerized Cotton, Size 40: 2 balls of white
Five Size 0 double-pointed knitting needles
Size 9 steel crochet hook

Abbreviations: Page 217.

INSTRUCTIONS

Starting at center, cast on 4 sts.

Row 1: Working with 2 needles only, **(k in front and in back of next st—inc made)** 4 times—8 sts.

continued

CROCHET FLORAL AFGHAN

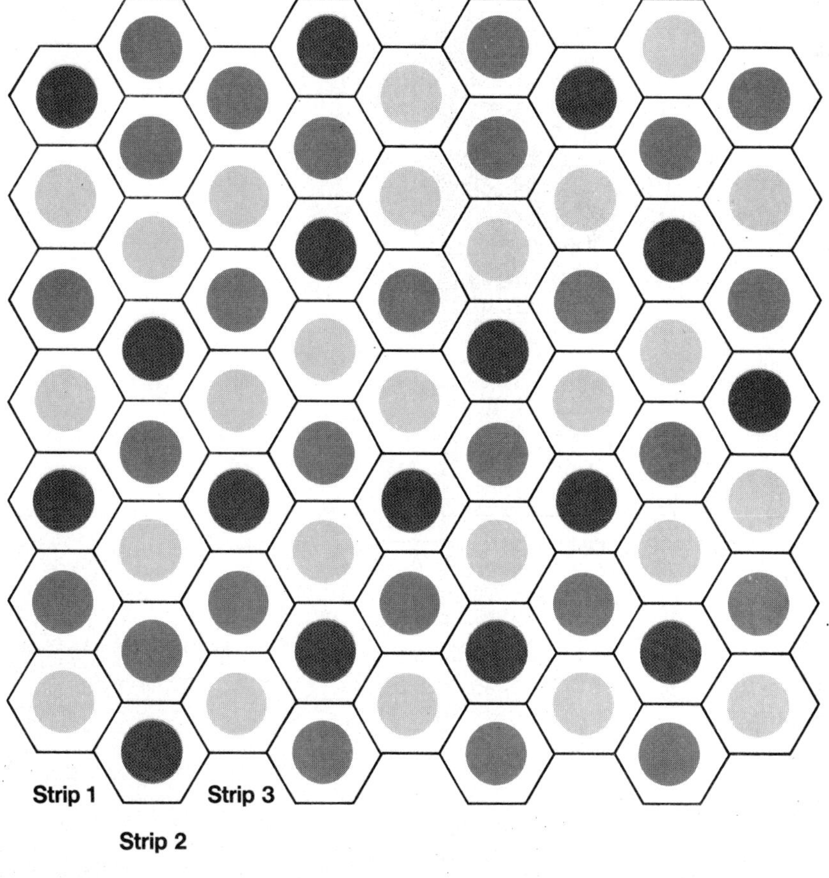

Note: The number of sts given at the end of each row or rnd indicates number of sts *on each needle.*

Change to work in rnds. *Foundation Rnd:* * With next needle (k 1, yo) twice; rep from * 3 times more—4 sts on each needle, counting each yo as a st. (*Note:* All yo's are counted and worked as sts.) Be careful not to twist sts and not to lose yo's at end of rnds.

Rnd 1: * Inc 1 st in next st, yo twice, drop next yo; rep from * around—8 sts.

Rnd 2: * (K 1, yo) twice, drop next 2 yo's; rep from * around—8 sts.

Rnd 3: * K 1, yo, drop next yo; rep from * around—8 sts.

Rnd 4: * Inc in next st, yo, drop next yo; rep from * around—12 sts.

Rnd 5: * K 2, k next yo; rep from * around—12 sts.

Rnds 6-8: K—12 sts.

Rnd 9: * K 2 tog, yo, k 1, yo; rep from * around—16 sts.

Rnd 10: * K 1, yo twice; drop next yo; rep from * around—24 sts.

Rnd 11: * K 1, yo, k next yo, drop next yo; rep from * around—24 sts.

Rnd 12: * K 1, ** yo, drop next yo, k 2; rep from ** across to last 2 sts on needle, end with yo, drop next yo, k 1. Rep from * for each needle—24 sts.

Rnd 13: * K 1, ** yo, k the yo, k 2; rep from ** across to last 2 sts on needle, end with yo, k the yo, k 1. Rep from * for each needle—32 sts.

Rnd 14: * K 1 (yo, k next yo, k 2 tog, k 1) 3 times; yo twice, (k next yo, k 2 tog, k 1, yo) 3 times; k next yo, k 2 tog, k 1, yo twice; k next yo, k 2 tog. Rep from * for each needle—34 sts.

Rnd 15: * K 1, (k next yo; k 3) twice; k next yo, k 2, inc in next st, k in front lp of next yo, k in back lp of following yo, inc in next st, k 2, (k next yo, k 3) twice; k next yo, k 2, inc in next st, k in front lp of next yo, k in back lp of following yo, inc in next st, k 1. Rep from * for each needle—38 sts.

Rnds 16-18: K all sts.

[With fourth needle, k first 4 sts on first needle, then sl first 4 sts from second needle onto first needle, sl first 4 sts of third needle onto second needle, slip first 4 sts from fourth needle onto third needle—38 sts on each needle.]

Note: For Rnds 19-27, work the directions as given twice across each of the 4 needles. The number of sts given at the end of a rnd indicates the number of sts on *each* needle.

Rnd 19: K 19, yo 5 times—48 sts.

Rnd 20: Sl 1, k 1, psso, k 15, k 2 tog, yo twice; drop next 2 yo, k in back lp of next yo, yo twice; drop next 2 yo—44 sts.

Rnd 21: K 17, yo, drop next yo, k in back lp of next yo, k 1, k in back lp of next yo, yo, drop next yo—44 sts.

Rnd 22: Sl 1, k 1, psso, k 13, k 2 tog, yo 3 times; drop next yo, sl 1, k 2 tog, psso, yo 3 times; drop next yo—44 sts

Rnd 23: K 15, **yo, drop next yo, k in back lp of next yo, yo, drop next yo—3 consecutive yo's worked.** K 1, work next 3 consecutive yo's as above—44 sts.

Rnd 24: Sl 1, k 1, psso, k 11, k 2 tog, yo, k in back lp of next yo, k 1, k in back lp of next yo, yo, k 1, yo, k in back lp of next yo, k 1, k in back lp of next yo, yo—48 sts.

Rnd 25: K 13, yo 4 times; drop next yo, sl 1, k 2 tog, psso, yo 3 times; drop next yo, k 1, yo 3 times; drop next yo, sl 1, k 2 tog, psso, yo 4 times, drop next yo—60 sts.

Rnd 26: Sl 1, k 1, psso, * yo twice, k l; rep from * 8 times more; yo twice, k 2 tog, yo 4 times, **(k in back lp of next yo, k in front lp of following yo) twice—4 consecutive yo's worked.** K 1, work next 3 consecutive yo's as above, k 1, work next 3 consecutive yo's as above, k 1, work next 4 consecutive yo's as above, yo 4 times—112 sts.

Rnd 27: (Sl next st onto right-hand needle, drop next 2 yo) 10 times; sl next st to right needle, sl the 11 slipped sts back to left needle and k the 11 sts tog to complete petal; work next 4 consecutive yo's as above, k 17, work next 4 consecutive yo's as above—52 sts.

Rnds 28-30: Knit—52 sts.

Rnd 31: * K 2 tog, yo twice; sl 1, k 1, psso; rep from * around—52 sts.

Rnd 32: Yo, * sl 1, k 1, psso, k 2 tog, yo twice; rep from * to last 4 sts of rnd, sl 1, k 1, psso, k 2 tog, yo—52 sts.

Rnds 33-34: Rep Rnds 31-32—52 sts.

Rnd 35: * K next yo, k 2, ** k next yo, drop following yo, k 2 tog, (k next yo, drop next yo, k 2) twice. Rep from ** across to last st on needle, end k next yo; rep from * for each rem needle—36 sts.

Rnds 36-62: Rep Rnds 6-32, rep instructions as often as needed on each needle. Number of sts on each needle at end of these repeated rnds is as follows: Rnds 6-8, 36 sts; Rnd 9, 48 sts; Rnds 10-12, 72 sts; Rnd 13, 96 sts; Rnd 14, 102 sts; Rnds 15-18, 114 sts.

Redistribute sts on needles following directions in [ ]s as indicated at end of Rnd 18—114 sts. Rnd 19—144 sts, Rnds 20-23—132 sts, Rnd 24—144 sts, Rnd 25—180 sts, Rnd 26—336 sts, Rnds 27-32—156 sts (62 rnds completed).

Rnds 63-66: Rep Rnds 31 and 32 alternately—156 sts.

Rnd 67: Rep Rnd 31—156 sts.

Rnd 68: * K 1, k in front lp of next yo, k in back lp of following yo, k 1, yo; rep from * around—195 sts.

Rnd 69: * K 4, yo, drop next yo. Rep from * around—195 sts.

Rnd 70: * (Sl next st to crochet hook) 4 times. Yo hook and draw lp through all 5 lps on hook, drop next yo, ch 12; rep from * around. Join. Fasten off.

Draw center together and secure. Block.

Flower Ring Doily

Shown on page 165.
Finished doily measures 11½ inches in diameter.

MATERIALS
DMC Cébélia, Size 10 (282-yard ball): 1 ball
Size 7 steel crochet hook

Abbreviations: Page 211.

INSTRUCTIONS
Beg at center, ch 7, join with sl st to form ring.

Rnd 1: Ch 1, * sc in ring, ch 1, 3 dc in ring, ch 1; rep from * around until 5 petals made; end ch 1, join with sl st to first sc. Sl st to first dc of next petal.

Rnd 2: Ch 7, * sk dc, dc in next dc, ch 4, dc in first dc of next petal, ch 4; rep from * around; end ch 4, join to third ch of beg ch-7—10 sps; fasten off.

For the flower ring
FIRST FLOWER, *Rnd 3:* Ch 7, join with sl st to form ring; rep Rnd 1, *above,* until 3 petals made; work the fourth petal until 2 dc are made, sl st in any ch-4 sp of center (Rnd 2); complete fourth petal; work the fifth petal until there are 2 dc, sl st in next ch-4 sp of Rnd 2, complete the petal. End ch 1, join to first sc; fasten off.

SECOND FLOWER: Work same as First Flower until third petal has 2 dc, sl st in center dc of first petal of First Flower, complete petal; work fourth petal until 2 dc are made, sl st in same ch-4 sp of Rnd 2 as last petal of last flower, complete petal; work fifth petal until 2 dc are made, sl st in next ch-4 sp of Rnd 2, complete flower as established.

Continue making and joining flowers same as Second Flower until there are 9 flowers. Join last flower as follows: Work flower until 2 dc of second petal are made, sl st to center dc of first petal of eighth flower, complete petal, work third petal until 2 dc are made, sl st in same ch-4 sp as for eighth flower, complete petal; work fourth petal until 2 dc are made, sl st in next ch-4 sp, complete petal; work fifth petal until 2 dc are made, sl st in center dc of third petal of First Flower, complete petal, join to first sc; do not fasten off.

Rnd 4: Sl st to center dc of next petal of last flower; ch 7, * trc in first dc of next petal of same flower, ch 4, trc in third dc of next petal of next flower, ch 4, dc in center of next petal of same flower, ch 4; rep from * around; end ch 4, join with sl st to third ch of beg ch-7.

Rnd 5: Ch 9, * trc in next st, ch 5; rep from * around; end ch 5, join to fourth ch of beg ch-9.

Rnd 6: Ch 5, * dc in third ch of next ch-5 lp, ch 2, dc in next trc, ch 2; rep from * around; end ch 3, join to third ch of beg ch-5—54 sps.

Rnd 7: Ch 3, dc in same st as join, * ch 4, sk next 2 ch-2 sps, in next ch-2 sp work dc, ch 5, dc; ch 4, sk next 2 ch-2 sps, 2 dc in next dc; rep from * around until 4 sps rem; ch 4, sk next 2 ch-2 sps, in next *dc* work dc, ch 5, dc; ch 4, join to top of beg ch.

Rnd 8: Ch 3, dc in same st as join, dc in next dc, * ch 4, sk next ch-lp, 9 dc in next ch-5 lp, ch 4, 2 dc in next dc, dc in next dc; rep from * around; end ch 4, join to top of beg ch.

Rnd 9: Ch 3, 2 dc in next dc, dc in next dc, * ch 4, sc in each of 9 dc, ch 4, dc in next dc, 2 dc in next dc, dc in next dc; rep from * around; end ch 4, join to top of beg ch.

Rnd 10: Ch 3, dc in next 3 dc, * ch 4, sc in each of 9 sc, ch 4, dc in next 4 dc; rep from * around; end ch 4, join to top of beg ch.

Rnd 11: Ch 3, dc in next dc, * ch 2, dc in next 2 dc, ch 4, **draw up lp in each of first 2 sc, yo, draw through 3 lps—dec made;** sc in next 5 sc, dec over last 2 sc; ch 4, dc in next 2 dc; rep from * around; end ch 4, join to top of beg ch.

Rnd 12: Ch 3, dc in next dc, * ch 5, dc in next 2 dc, ch 5, sc in 7 sc, ch 5, dc in next 2 dc; rep from * around; end ch 5, join to beg ch.

Rnd 13: Ch 3, dc in next dc, * ch 5, sc in next ch-5 lp, ch 5, dc in next 2 dc, ch 5, dec over first 2 sc, sc in 3 sc, dec over last 2 sc, ch 5, dc in next 2 dc; rep from * around; end ch 5, join as above.

Rnd 14: Ch 3, dc in next dc, * (ch 5, sc in next ch-5 lp) twice, ch 5, dc in next 2 dc, ch 5, sc in 5 sc, ch 5, dc in next 2 dc; rep from * around; end with ch 5, join.

Rnd 15: Ch 3, dc in next dc, * (ch 5, sc in next ch-5 lp) 3 times; ch 5, dc in next 2 dc, ch 5, dec over first 2 sc, sc in next sc, dec over last 2 sc, ch 5, dc in next 2 dc; rep from * around; end with ch 5, join.

Rnd 16: Ch 3, dc in next dc, * (ch 5, sc in next ch-5 lp) 4 times; ch 5, dc in next 2 dc, ch 5, sc in 3 sc, ch 5, dc in next 2 dc; rep from * around; end ch 5, join.

Rnd 17: Ch 3, dc in next dc, * (ch 5, sc in next ch-5 lp) 3 times; ch 5, sc in same lp as last sc, (ch 5, sc in next ch-5 lp) twice; ch 5, dc in next 2 dc, ch 5, draw up lp in each of 3 sc, yo and draw through all lps; ch 5, dc in next dc, sl st in sp between the 2 previous dc, dc in next dc; rep from * around; end ch 5, join to top of beg ch, sl st in sp between 2 previous dc; fasten off.

FINISHING: Lightly starch and block to shape.

Scallop Edge Doily

Shown on page 165.
Doily is 13¼ inches in diameter.

MATERIALS
DMC Cébélia, Size 10 (282-yard ball): 1 ball
Size 7 steel crochet hook

Abbreviations: Page 211.

INSTRUCTIONS
Beg at center, ch 7, join with sl st to form ring. *Rnd 1:* Ch 4, trc in ring, * ch 2, 2 trc in ring; rep from * 7 times more; ch 2, join with sl st to top of ch-4—9 ch-2 sps made.

continued

Rnd 2: Ch 4, trc in next trc, * ch 5, trc in next 2 trc; rep from * around; end ch 5, join with sl st to top of ch-4; fasten off.

Begin to work ring of shells as follows:

Rnd 3: **Ch 4, in fourth ch from hook work dc, ch 2, 2 dc—beg shell made;** ch 2, with right side facing, sl st in any ch-5 sp of Rnd 2, ch 2, *turn;* in ch-2 sp of beg shell work **2 dc, ch 2, 2 dc—shell made;** ch 5, *turn;* * shell in ch-2 sp of previous shell, ch 2, sk next trc of Rnd 2, sl st in next trc of Rnd 2, ch 2, *turn;* (shell in shell, ch 5, *turn;* shell in shell, ch 2, sl st in next ch-5 sp of Rnd 2, ch 2, *turn*) 3 times; shell in shell, ch 5, *turn.* Rep from * one more time, then rep from * again, *except* work through set of ( )s just twice; end 2 dc in ch-2 sp of previous shell, ch 1, sl st in beg ch at base of beg shell, ch 1, 2 dc in same ch-2 sp as last 2 dc, ch 1, *turn;* join with a trc in top of beg ch-4—24 shells made.

Rnd 4: Ch 8, sc in sp made by ch-1 and trc, ch 8, sc in same sp, * ch 4, 10 dc in next ch-5 lp, ch 4, sc in next ch-5 lp, (ch 8, sc in same sp) twice; rep from * around; end ch 4, join to first ch of beg ch-8. Sl st in each ch to center of ch-8 lp.

Rnd 5: Ch 3, dc in same lp, * ch 5, 2 dc in next ch-8 lp, ch 5, sc in next 10 dc, ch 5, 2 dc in next ch-8 lp; rep from * around; end sc in 10 dc, ch 5, join to top of beg ch-3.

Rnd 6: Ch 3, dc in next dc, * ch 5, sc in next ch-5 lp, ch 5, dc in next 2 dc, ch 5, sc in 10 sc, ch 5, dc in next 2 dc; rep from * around; end ch 5, join to top of beg ch-3.

Rnd 7: Ch 3, dc in next dc, * (ch 5, sc in next lp) twice; ch 5, dc in next 2 dc, ch 5; **draw up a lp in each of first 2 sc, yo and draw through all lps—dec made;** sc in next 6 sc, dec over last 2 sc, ch 5, dc in next 2 dc; rep from * around; end ch 5, join to top of beg ch-3.

Rnd 8: Ch 3, dc in next dc, * (ch 5, sc in next lp) 3 times; ch 5, dc in next 2 dc, ch 5, dec over first 2 sc, sc in 4 sc, dec over last 2 sc, ch 5, dc in next 2 dc; rep from * around; end ch 5, join same as Rnd 7.

Rnd 9: Ch 3, dc in next dc, * (ch 5, sc in next lp) 4 times; ch 5, dc in next 2 dc, ch 5, dec over first 2 sc, sc in 2 sc, dec over last 2 sc, ch 5, dc in next 2 dc; rep from * around; end ch 5, join.

Rnd 10: Ch 3, dc in next dc, * (ch 5, sc in next lp) 5 times; ch 5, dc in next 2 dc, ch 5, sk next sc, sc in 3 sc, ch 5, dc in next 2 dc; rep from * around; end ch 5, join.

Rnd 11: Ch 3, dc in next dc, * (ch 5, dc in next lp) 6 times; ch 5, dc in next 2 dc, sk next grp of 3 sc, dc in next 2 dc; rep from * around; end dc in last 2 dc, join to beg ch-3.

Rnd 12: Ch 1, sc in next dc, * (ch 2, sc in center ch of next ch-5 lp, ch 2, sc in next dc) 7 times; sk next 2 dc, sc in next dc; rep from * around; end sc in dc, sk last dc; join to first sc.

Rnd 13: Ch 1, sc in same st as join, * (ch 2, sc in next sc) 13 times; ch 2, sk next sc, sc in next sc; rep from * around; end ch 2, sk last sc, join to beg sc.

Rnd 14: Sl st in each ch to next sc, ch 7, * (trc in next sc, ch 3) 11 times; trc in next sc, sk next sc, trc in next sc, ch 3; rep from * around; end with trc, join to fourth ch of beg ch-7.

Rnd 15: Ch 1, sc in same st as join, * (ch 3, sc in next trc) 11 times; ch 3, sk next trc, sc in next trc; rep from * around; end ch 3, join to first sc at beg of rnd.

Rnd 16: Ch 1, sc in same st as join, ch 3, * sc in next sc, ch 3; rep from * around; end ch 3, sk trc, join to first sc at beg of rnd.

Rnd 17: Ch 6, * dc in next sc, ch 3; rep from * around; end ch 3, join to third ch of beg ch.

Rnd 18: **Ch 4, holding last 2 lps of each st on hook, work 2 trc in same ch as joining, yo and draw through all lps—beg cl made;** ch 4, **holding last 2 lps of each st on hook, work 3 trc in same ch as beg cl, yo and draw through all lps—cl made;** ch 4, cl in same ch, * ch 1, (dc in next dc, ch 3) twice; dc in next dc, ch 1, in next dc work (cl, ch 4, cl, ch 4, cl); rep from * around; end dc in last dc, sc in top of beg cl to join.

Rnd 19: Ch 6, * (dc in next ch-4 lp, ch 3) twice; dc in next dc, ch 4, sc in next dc, ch 4, dc in next dc, ch 3; rep from * around; end ch 4, join with sl st to third ch of beg ch-6.

Rnd 20: Ch 1, 4 sc in each ch-lp around; join with sl st to first sc.

Rnd 21: Ch 1, sc in each sc around, join; fasten off.

FINISHING: Lightly starch and block to shape.

Fleur-de-Lis Doily

Shown on page 165.
Finished size of doily is 13 inches in diameter.

MATERIALS

DMC Cébélia, Size 10 (282-yard ball): 1 ball
Size 7 steel crochet hook

Abbreviations: Page 211.

INSTRUCTIONS

Beg at center, ch 7, join with sl st to form ring.

Rnd 1: Ch 1, * sc in ring, ch 1, 3 dc in ring, ch 1; rep from * around until 5 petals are made; end ch 1, join with sl st to first sc. Sl st in next ch and next 2 dc.

Rnd 2: Ch 7, * trc in next sc between petals, ch 4, dc in center dc of next petal, ch 4; rep from * around; end ch 4, join with sl st in third ch of beg ch-7.

Rnd 3: Ch 1, sc in same place as join, * ch 4, **holding last 2 lps of each st on hook, work 3 trc in next trc, yo and draw through all lps on hook—cl made;** (ch 4, cl in same st as last cl) twice, ch 4, sc in next dc; rep from * around, ending with ch 4, join to first sc.

Rnd 4: Ch 9, dc in top of next cl; (ch 5, dc in top of next cl) twice; * ch 5, trc in next sc, (ch 5, dc in top of next cl) 3 times; rep from * around; ending with ch 5, join in fourth ch of beg ch-9.

Rnd 5: Ch 9, dc in next dc, (ch 5, dc in next dc) twice; * ch 5, trc in next trc, (ch 5, dc in next dc) 3 times; rep from * around; end ch 5, join in fourth ch of beg ch-9.

Rnd 6: **Ch 4, holding last 2 lps of each st on hook, work 2 trc in same ch as joining, yo and draw through all lps—beg cl made;** ch 4, in same ch work (cl, ch 4, cl); * ch 3, trc in next dc, (ch 5, trc in next dc) twice; ch 3, in next tr work (cl, ch 4, cl, ch 4, cl); rep from * around; end ch 3, join to top of beg ch-4.

Rnd 7: Ch 8, trc in top of next cl, ch 4, trc in top of next cl, * ch 4, trc in next trc, (ch 5, trc in next trc) twice; (ch 4, trc in top of next cl) 3 times; rep from * around; end trc in last trc, ch 4, join in fourth ch of beg ch-8.

Rnd 8: Ch 6, * dc in next ch-sp, ch 3, dc in next trc, ch 3; rep from * around; end ch 3, join to third ch of beg ch-6—60 ch-3 sps.

Rnd 9: Ch 3, dc in same ch as joining, * ch 5, sk next 2 ch-3 lps, in center ch of next ch-3 lp work (dc, ch 5, dc); ch 5, sk next 2 ch-3 lps, 2 dc in next dc; rep from * around; end ch 5, sk last 2 sps, join in top of beg ch-3.

Rnd 10: Ch 3, dc in next dc, * ch 5, sk next ch-5 lp, 11 dc in next ch-5 lp, ch 5, sk next ch-5 lp, dc in next 2 dc; rep from * around; end ch 5, sk last ch-5 lp, join in top of beg ch-3.

Rnd 11: Ch 3, dc in next dc, * ch 5, sc in each of next 11 dc, ch 5, dc in next 2 dc; rep from * around; end ch 5, join to beg ch-3.

Rnd 12: Ch 3, dc in same st used for join, ch 2, 2 dc in next dc, * ch 5, sc in 11 sc, ch 5, 2 dc in next dc, ch 2, 2 dc in next dc; rep from * around; end ch 5, join to beg ch-3.

Rnd 13: Ch 3, dc in next dc, ch 5, dc in next 2 dc, * ch 5, sk next sc, sc in next 9 sc, ch 5, dc in next 2 dc, ch 5, dc in next 2 dc; rep from * around; end ch 5, join to top of ch-3.

Rnd 14: Ch 3, dc in next dc, * ch 5, sc in next ch-5 lp, ch 5, dc in next 2 dc, ch 5, sc in 9 sc, ch 5, dc in next 2 dc; rep from * around; end ch 5, join to top of ch-3.

Rnd 15: Ch 3, dc in next dc, * (ch 5, sc in next ch-5 lp) twice; ch 5, dc in next 2 dc, ch 5, sk next sc, sc in 7 sc, ch 5, dc in next 2 dc; rep from * around; end sc in 7 sc, ch 5, join.

Rnd 16: Ch 3, dc in next dc, * (ch 5, sc in next ch-5 lp) twice; ch 8, sc in same lp, ch 5, sc in next ch-5 lp, ch 5, dc in next 2 dc, ch 5, sk next sc, sc in 5 sc, ch 5, dc in next 2 dc; rep from * around; end sc in 5 sc, ch 5, join.

Rnd 17: Ch 3, dc in next dc, * (ch 5, sc in next ch-lp) 3 times; ch 5, sc in same lp, (ch 5, sc in next ch-lp) twice; ch 5, dc in next 2 dc, ch 5, sk next sc, sc in 3 sc, ch 5, dc in next 2 dc; rep from * around; end sc in 3 sc, ch 5, join; fasten off.

FINISHING: Lightly starch and block to shape.

Filet Crochet Pillow

Shown on page 167.

Pillow is 15 inches square.

MATERIALS

J. & P. Coats Knit-Cro-Sheen: 2 balls of No. 42 cream

Size 7 steel crochet hook, or size to obtain gauge given below

½ yard of 44-inch-wide medium-weight fabric

Polyester fiberfill

Sewing thread to match fabric

Abbreviations: Page 211.

Gauge: 4 blocks = 1 inch; 4 rows = 1 inch.

INSTRUCTIONS

Starting at lower edge, ch 128.

Row 1 (right side): Dc in eighth ch from hook—starting sp made; * **ch 2, sk 2 ch, dc in next ch—sp made;** rep from * across—41 sps; ch 5, turn.

Row 2: **Sk first dc, dc in next dc—starting sp over sp made; * ch 2, sk 2 ch, dc in next dc—sp over sp made;** rep from * to last sp; **ch 2, sk next 2 ch of turning ch, dc in next ch—end sp made;** ch 5, turn.

Row 3: Sk first dc, dc in next dc, ch 2, dc in next dc; * **2 dc in next sp, dc in next dc—bl over sp made;** rep from * to last 2 sps; ch 2, dc in next dc, ch 2, sk 2 ch of turning ch, dc in next ch, ch 5, turn.

Row 4: Sk first dc, dc in next dc, ch 2, dc in next dc; **dc in each of next 3 dc—bl over bl made; (ch 2, sk 2 dc, dc in next dc—sp over bl made)** 35 times, 1 bl, 1 sp, 1 end sp.

Rows 5-10: Work from chart, page 176, through Row 10, reading even-numbered rows from left to right and odd-numbered rows from right to left. At end of Row 10, ch 35.

Row 11: Working over the 35 chs, dc in eighth ch from hook, (ch 2, sk 2 ch, dc in next ch) 8 times, ch 2, sk 2 ch, dc in next dc—10 sps inc. Working across piece already established make 2 sps, 1 bl, 5 sps, 1 bl, 23 sps, 1 bl, 5 sps, 1 bl, 2 sps; **ch 5, dc in base of last dc—sp inc,** (ch 5, turn, dc in center ch of ch-5 lp) 9 times—10 sps inc. Ch 5.

Row 12: Working in same st used to work incs, dc in next st, (ch 2, dc in next st) 9 times. Continue over piece working 2 sps, 1 bl, 5 sps, 1 bl, 23 sps, 1 bl, 5 sps, 1 bl, 12 sps. Ch 5, turn.

Continue from chart until Row 53 is completed; do not ch 5 at end of Row 53; fasten off, turn.

Sk first 10 sps, join thread in top of dc at beg of next sp, ch 5, dc in next dc. Continue to work from chart, leaving 10 sps unworked at end of Row 54. Fasten off at end of Row 63.

continued

FILET CROCHET PILLOW

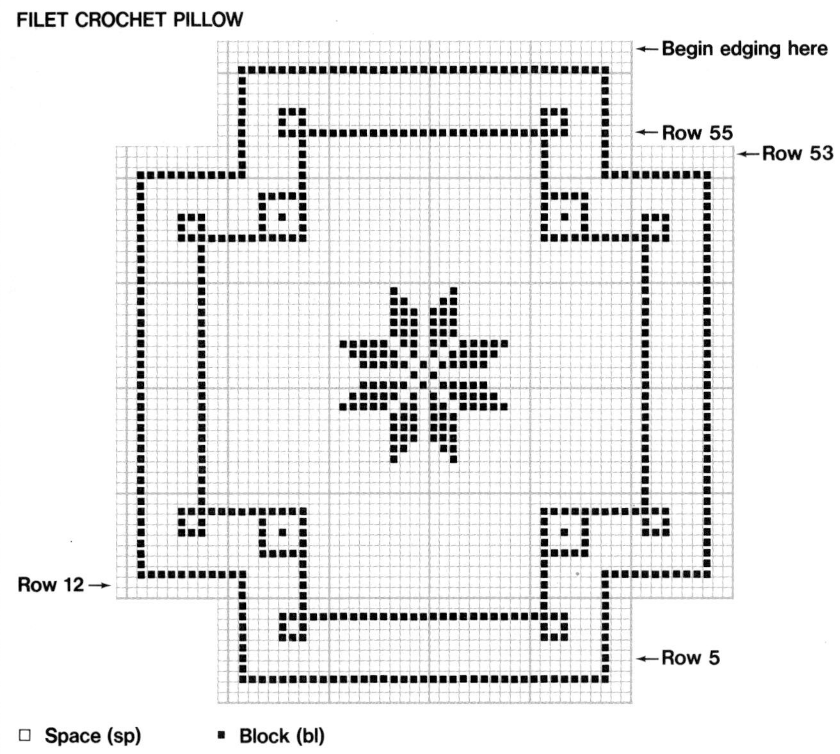

EDGING: *Rnd 1:* Attach thread in top right corner sp, ch 3, in same sp work 2 dc, ch 2, 3 dc, ch 2, sk next sp; * 3 dc in next ch-2 sp, ch 2, sk next sp; rep from * to corner sp. In corner sp work 3 dc, ch 2, 3 dc; ch 2, sk next sp. Rep from first * 3 times; 3 dc in next sp, sk last sp on side and first sp on next side at inner corner; rep from first * to next corner sp. In outer corner sp work 3 dc, ch 2, 3 dc. Work the rem sides to correspond; join last ch-2 to top of ch-3 at beg of rnd.

Rnd 2: Sl st in next 2 dc and into ch-2 sp, ch 3, in corner sp make 2 dc, ch 2, 3 dc; ch 2, * 3 dc in next ch-2 sp, ch 2; rep from * to next corner, in corner lp work 3 dc, ch 2, 3 dc; ch 2, rep from * to within last ch-2 lp at inner corner, 3 dc in last ch-3 lp, 3 dc in first ch-2 lp on next side; rep from first * to next corner; in corner ch-2 sp work 3 dc, ch 2, 3 dc.

Work rem sides to correspond; join to top of ch-3 at beg of rnd.

Rnd 3: * **Ch 5, sl st in third ch from hook—picot made;** ch 2, sc in corner lp, ** make picot, ch 2, sc in next ch-2 sp; rep from ** to next corner. Rep from * around to correspond; join last ch-2 to first ch at beg of rnd; fasten off.

When assembling pillow, use doily as pattern for cutting out pillow front and back. Trace around doily onto a sheet of paper; add ½-inch seam margins and cut out pattern.

Cut pillow front and back from fabric. With right sides facing, sew around three sides. Turn, press, and stuff with fiberfill. Slip-stitch fourth side closed. Slip-stitch doily to one side of pillow.

Filet Crochet Rose Edging

Shown on pages 166–167.
Finished lace is approximately 10½ inches deep; one pattern repeat is approximately 10½ inches wide.

MATERIALS

American Thread Gem crochet cotton, Size 30 (350-yard ball): 1 ball for 10 inches of lace

Size 10 steel crochet hook, or size to obtain gauge given below

Abbreviations: Page 211.

Gauge: 7 sps = 1 inch; 7 rows = 1 inch.

INSTRUCTIONS

Ch 127. *Row 1:* Dc in fourth ch from hook and in next 3 ch; (ch 1, sk ch, dc in next ch) 59 times; dc in last 2 ch; ch 3, turn.

Row 2: **Sk first dc, dc in next 2 dc—beg bl over bl made; (ch 1, dc in next dc—sp over sp made)** 59 times; **dc in next 2 dc—bl over bl made; dc in next dc and in top of turning ch—end bl over bl made.** Ch 6, turn.

Row 3: **Dc in fourth ch from hook, dc in next 2 chs and in next dc—2-bl inc made; (ch 1, sk 1 dc, dc in next dc—sp over bl made)** twice; work 25 more sps, **(dc in next sp, dc in next dc—bl over sp made)** 6 times; work 28 sps, work end bl; ch 3, turn.

Rows 4–7: Work from chart, *opposite. Row 8:* Work from chart to A, ch 5, sk 1 dc, dc in next dc, dc in next sp, dc in next dc, sp, 4 bl, sp, bl, end bl. Ch 6, turn.

Row 9: Work a 2-bl inc, 4 sp, 2 bl, sp, bl, ch 5, sc in ch-5 lp, ch 5, sk 2 dc, dc in next dc, dc in next sp, dc in next dc, complete row from chart. Ch 3, turn. *Row 10:* Work chart to B, ch 5, sc in first ch-5 lp, ch 5, sc in next ch-5 lp, ch 5, sk 2 dc, dc in next dc, dc in next sp, dc in next dc, 6 sp, bl, end bl. Ch 3, turn.

FILET CROCHET ROSE EDGING

— Row 72

— Row 1

B | A

C

□ Space (sp) ■ Block (bl)

Row 11: Sk 1 dc, dc in next 4 dc, 4 sp, 2 bl, sp, 2 dc in first ch-5 lp, ch 5, sc in next ch-5 lp, ch 5, 2 dc in following ch-5 lp, dc in next dc, complete row following chart. Ch 3, turn. *Row 12:* Work from chart to C, 2 dc in first ch-5 lp, ch 1, 2 dc in next ch-5 lp, dc in next dc, sp, 4 bl, sp, 2 bl. **Do not work in last 3 dc and turning ch—2 bl dec at end of row made.** Ch 3, turn.

Using chart, continue through Row 72. Rep Rows 1–72 for pat for desired length; fasten off. Wash, starch, and block lace; machine-sew to fabric item.

HEART EDGING

Heart Edging

Shown on pages 166–167. Tablecloth is approximately 53 inches square, including lace.

MATERIALS

Clark's Big Ball crochet cotton, Size 30: 5 balls, white
Size 12 steel crochet hook, or size to obtain gauge given below
1⅓ yards of tablecloth fabric

Abbreviations: Page 211.
Gauge: 15 dc = 1 inch; one heart motif repeat = 3¼ inches.

INSTRUCTIONS

The cloth shown features thirteen 3¼-inch-wide motif repeats along each side. Therefore, the finished size of the fabric insertion is 42¼ inches square. If you would like to make this cloth larger or smaller, decrease or increase the length of each side of the fabric insertion in multiples of 3¼ inches. You may add this edging to purchased curtains or those you've sewn yourself. Carefully measure the sides of the curtain panels and plan the heart repeat motif in multiples of 3¼ inches.

EDGING: Ch 54. *Row 1:* Dc in fourth ch from hook and in each of next 2 ch—1 starting bl made; (ch 2, sk 2 ch, dc in next ch) 5 times—5 sp made; dc in next 3 ch, (ch 2, sk 2 ch, dc in next ch) 10 times—10 sp made; [ch 8, turn; dc in 6th, 7th, and 8th ch from hook, dc in last dc of previous row].

Row 2: (Ch 2, dc in next dc) 3 times; (2 dc in next sp, dc in next dc) 3 times; (ch 2, dc in next dc) 4 times; dc in next 3 dc, ch 2, dc in next dc, (2 dc in next sp, dc in next dc) 4 times; dc in next 2 dc and in top of ch-3; ch 3, turn.

Row 3: Sk first dc, dc in each of next 3 dc, (ch 2, sk 2 dc, dc in next

continued

dc) 3 times; dc in each of next 3 dc, ch 2, dc in each of next 4 dc, (ch 2, dc in next dc) 3 times; 2 dc in next sp, dc in each of next 10 dc, 2 dc in next sp, dc in next dc, (ch 2, dc in next dc) 2 times; ch 2, sk 2 dc, dc in next dc, 3 dc in ch-8 lp. Rep pat bet [ ]s of Row 1.

Refer to chart, page 177, for working Rows 4–8. Work the pat that appears in [ ]s at the end of Row 1 for ends of Rows 5 and 7.

Row 9: Sk first dc, dc in each of next 3 dc, ch 2, dc in next dc, (ch 2, sk 2 dc, dc in next dc) 4 times; dc in each of next 3 dc, (ch 2, dc in next dc) 4 times; ch 2, sk 2 dc, dc in next 7 dc, 2 dc in next sp, dc in next dc, (ch 2, dc in next dc) 2 times; ch 2, sk 2 dc, dc in each of next 7 dc, 2 dc in next sp, dc in next dc, (ch 2, dc in next dc) 2 times, ch 2, sk 2 dc, dc in next dc, 3 dc in ch-8 lp; [ch 4, turn, dc in fourth dc, 2 dc in next sp, dc in next dc].

Refer to the chart for the remainder of the pat. Work the pat that appears in [ ]s at the end of Row 9 for the ends of Rows 11, 13, and 15. Rep Rows 1 through 16 for pat.

TO MAKE A MESH CORNER: *Row 1:* Ch 5, sk first 3 dc, dc in next dc; (ch 2, sk next 2 dc or ch-2, dc in next 2 dc) 15 times; 2 dc in last ch-2 sp, dc in last dc, ch 3, turn.

Row 2: Sk first dc, dc in each of next 2 dc, (ch 2, sk next ch-2, dc in next dc) 15 times; ch 2, dc in third ch of ch-5 at beg of previous row, ch 5, turn.

Row 3: Dc in next dc, (ch 2, dc in next dc) 15 times; dc in each of next 3 dc, ch 3, turn. Rep Rows 2 and 3 alternately 7 times more.

Next row: Sk first dc, dc in each dc, and 2 dc in every ch-2 sp across row; fasten off.

TO BEGIN THE NEXT SIDE: Attach thread at the end of Row 16. Work Row 1 of pat, making each dc at right angles to the dc of the mesh corner and working groups of dc around the posts of the *turning* dc of the corner mesh block.

Rep until all four sides of the lace edging are completed. Slip-stitch the end of the fourth side to the end of the first side.

TO ASSEMBLE: Wash, starch, and block the lace. Pin it to the shape desired.

Measure the inside of the lace assembly for the fabric insertion, and hem a fabric square to this size. Hand-sew lace to the edge of the fabric insertion.

Tablecloth Edging

Shown on pages 166–167.
Finished depth of lace is about 8 inches; pattern repeat measures 6¾ inches wide.

MATERIALS

Bucilla Blue Label crochet cotton (400-yard skeins): 1 skein ivory (makes approximately 42 inches of lace)
Size 8 steel crochet hook

Abbreviations: Page 211.

INSTRUCTIONS

Using a single strand of cotton and steel hook, ch 60.

Row 1: Dc in fourth ch from hook, dc in next 2 chs; **ch 2, sk 2 ch, sc in next ch, ch 2, sk 2 ch, dc in next ch—V-st made; dc in next 6 chs—2 bl made,** (ch 2, sk 2 ch, dc in next ch) 6 times, 2 bl, 2 V-st, 2 bl; ch 3, turn.

Row 2: **Sk first dc, dc in next 6 dc—beg 2 bl over 2 bl made; (ch 5, sk V-st, dc in next dc—2 bl-sp over V-st made)** twice; **dc in next 6 dc—2 bl over 2 bl made; (ch 2, dc in next dc—sp over sp made)** 6 times; 2 bl over 2 bl, 2 bl-sp over V-st; **ch 2, dc in top of turning ch—end sp made.** Ch 3, turn.

Row 3: **Sk first dc, 2 dc in ch-2 sp, dc in next dc—beg bl over sp made; ch 2, sc in center ch of ch-5 lp, ch 2, dc in next dc—V-st over 2 bl-sp made; ch 2, sk 2 dc, sc in next dc, ch 2, sk 2 dc, dc in next dc—V-st over 2 bl made; (2 dc in ch-2 sp, dc in next dc—bl over sp made)** twice; 4 sps, **(ch 2, sk 2 dc, dc in next dc—sp over bl made)** twice; **5 dc in ch-5 lp, dc in next dc—2 bl over 2 bl-sp made;** work 2 V-sts, **(trc in side 2 lps at base of previous st) 6 times—2 bl inc at end of row made.** Ch 3, turn.

TABLECOTH EDGING

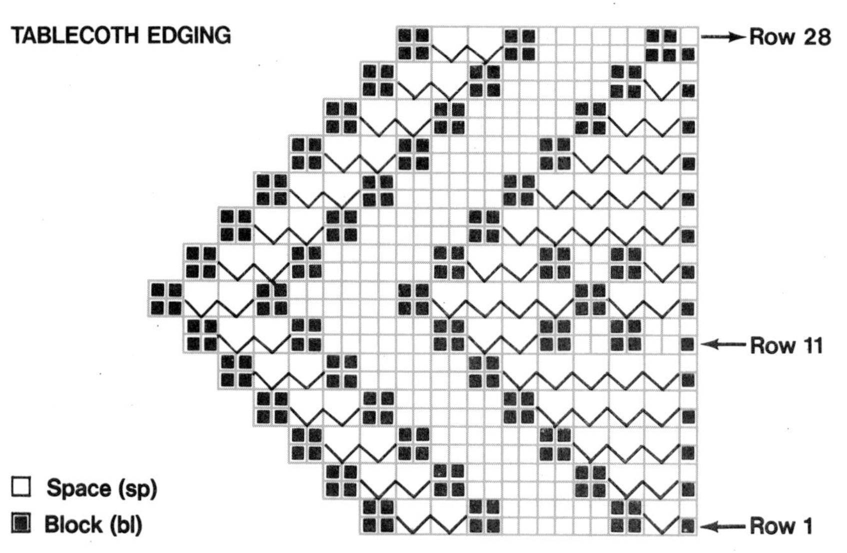

Continue working from chart, *opposite*, for Rows 4–10, stitching even-numbered rows from left to right and odd-numbered rows from right to left.

Row 11: Beg bl, V-st, 2 bl, **ch 2, dc in center of ch-5 lp, ch 2, dc in next dc—2 sps over 2 bl-sp made;** complete row following chart.

Rows 12, 13, 14, 16: Work from chart.

Row 15: Beg bl, V-st, 2 bl, 2 sp, 2 bl, 2 V-st, 2 bl, 6 sp, 2 bl, 2 V-st, 2 bl, ch 3, turn. **6 sts rem unworked—2 bl dec made.** Continue working from chart, repeat 2 bl dec at ends of Rows 17, 19, 21, 23, 25, and 27.

Rep Rows 1–28 for pat for desired length ending with Row 28. At end of Row 1, work dc in base of previous dc 6 times to establish work for Row 2. Fasten off, wash, starch, and block. Hand-stitch to fabric hem.

Filet Crochet Antimacassar

Shown on page 166.

MATERIALS
Clark's Big Ball crochet cotton, Size 30: 2 balls of white
Size 10 steel crochet hook

Abbreviations: Page 211.
Gauge: 5 bls or sps = 1 inch; 6 rows = 1 inch.

INSTRUCTIONS

Starting at lower edge, ch 54.

Row 1 (right side): **Dc in fourth ch from hook and in next 2 ch—starting block (bl) made; dc in next 3 ch—another bl made**; make 16 more bls (see chart, *right*), ch 17, turn. *Row 2:* Make starting bl and 4 more bls—5 bls inc at beg of row; complete row following chart.

Read chart from right to left, including *center,* then for remainder of row disregard *center,* and follow chart back again to right edge, increasing 5 bls at end of row.

Following chart, complete remainder of chair back.

FILET CROCHET ANTIMACASSAR

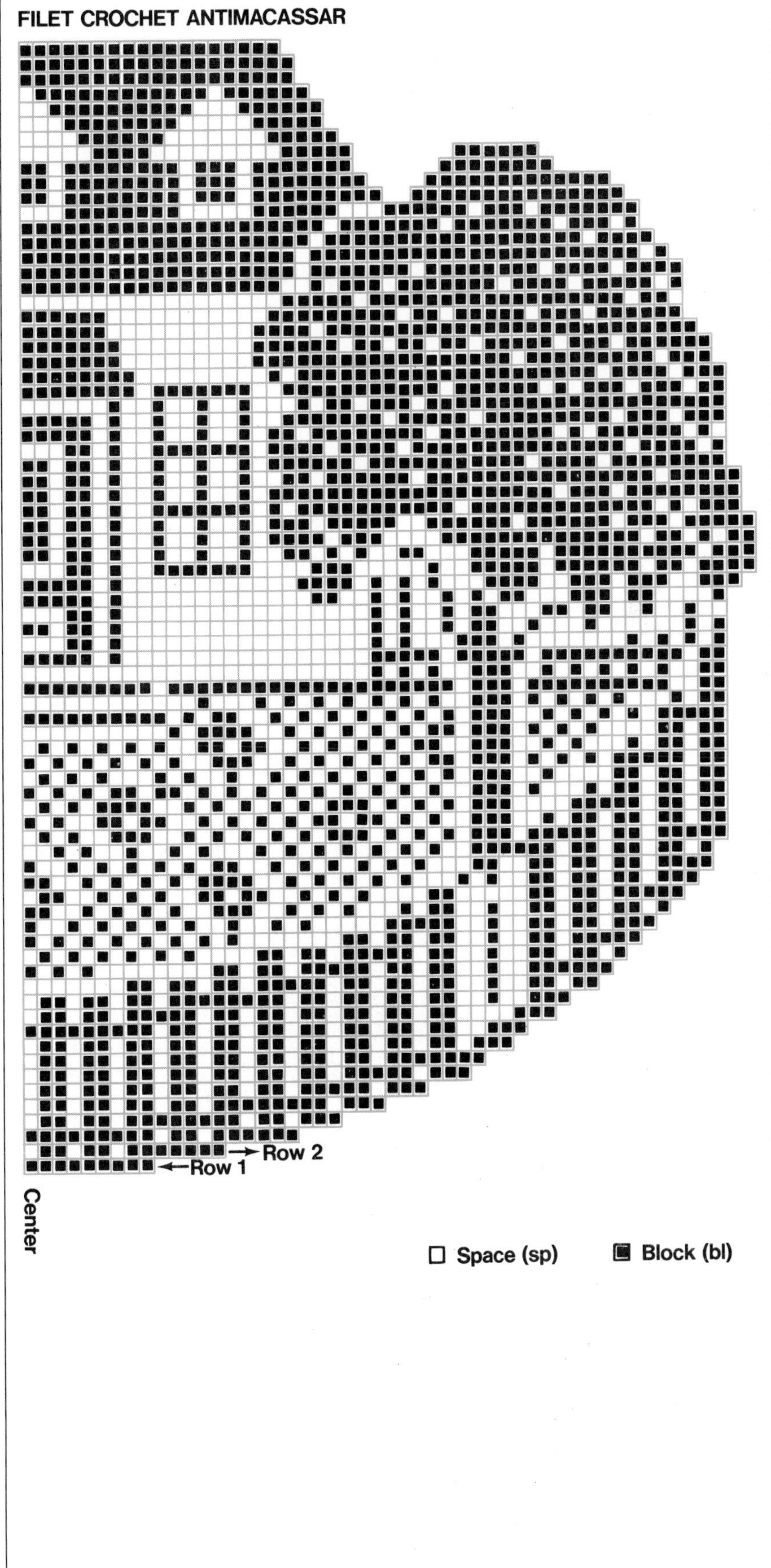

The Loveliness of Lace

LACY LOOKS TO WEAR AND ENJOY

Intricate openwork patterns create the luxurious look of lace for these enchanting wardrobe collectibles. Here and on the following pages you'll find an assortment of knitted and crocheted garments and accessories designed to delight the most ardent romantic.

Opulent texture and a lavish mix of patterns grace a cotton knit V-neck cardigan, *left.* A *tour de force* for experienced knitters, the sweater features diagonal rows of stockinette, reverse, openwork, and bobble patterns on the front and back sections, with horizontal bands of alternating patterns on the sleeves. Ruffled cuffs and a stylish peplum complete the design. Directions begin on page 188.

LACY LOOKS TO WEAR AND ENJOY

Here's a pair of fresh and flattering creations for the young at heart.

A deep cascade of crocheted lace, *right,* softens the neckline of a purchased V-neck sweater. Worked in a simple shell-stitch pattern, this graceful collar knows no season.

You'll want to wear this collar over a simple wool sweater or dress in the winter, then use it to dress up bright cotton knits in summer. For extra glamour, you might run rows of rich velvet, satin, or grosgrain ribbons through the mesh openings along the inside edge of the collar.

With minor alterations, this same shell-stitch pattern works into a flirty flounced edging of any desired depth and length. Stitched over a fabric ruffle in a boldly contrasting color, it would make a delightfully fanciful finish for a cotton petticoat skirt. You're sure to think of other appropriate uses.

The exquisite two-piece crocheted ensemble, *opposite,* is pretty enough for a wedding day. Made of graduating medallions, it features a flattering V-neckline with a softly ruffled collar and a scalloped finish for the capped sleeves and easy A-line skirt.

To show this delicate pattern to best advantage, wear the dress over a simple camisole slip in a lightly contrasting shade of taffeta.

As with other medallion patterns, the basic building block used for this dress is remarkably versatile. For example, you might assemble a number of the larger medallions to make an airy shawl in an interesting shape—square, rectangular, even triangular.

The medallion also is appropriate for traditional tablecloths, bedspreads, and doilies of any desired dimension. Or, you might work the design in worsted yarn for a sturdy country-style placemat

LACY LOOKS TO WEAR AND ENJOY

Delicate Irish crochet accessories, like the gloves, *above,* and the collar, *right* and *opposite,* add a touch of class to any outfit.

Created in the nineteenth century in imitation of popular (and expensive) Venetian point lace, Irish crochet is characterized by softly sculptured floral motifs set into backgrounds of crocheted mesh.

For traditional patterns such as this collar, work the floral motifs first, and baste them to a fabric ground. Then crochet the mesh around and between the blossoms and leaves.

For a more modern adaptation of the Irish crochet technique (see instructions for the gloves), crochet the mesh background separately. Then work the flowers, and appliqué them to the mesh.

Though clearly reminiscent of a more romantic era, both the gloves and the collar pictured on these pages make stunning accessories for contemporary wardrobes, too.

LACY LOOKS TO WEAR AND ENJOY

Inspired by the tablecloth and bedspread medallions of yesteryear, the filigree stole, *right,* is crocheted with summer-weight ecru cotton thread and trimmed with a fanciful eyelet ruffle.

For a cold weather version of this charming wrap, stitch the same pattern in soft wool yarn in a color of your choice. Then finish it with a handsome border of crocheted edging or a lavish spill of fringe.

Simple filet crochet worked in medium-weight cotton thread is ideal for a rose-pattern "morning coat," *opposite.* The long, lean styling, open front, and wide sleeves of this classic design are perfect foils for the lacy bodice and ruffled cuffs of an antique Victorian blouse.

The same jacket looks just as stylish over an elegant silk shirt or a cotton turtleneck. Or, slip it over a camisole for a stunning evening ensemble. The length of the jacket, of course, can be altered easily to suit your own individual proportions.

Once you've mastered the basics of charting filet crochet patterns, you'll find it easy and fun to combine motifs in new and intriguing ways. For example, you might substitute another favorite motif for the rose used here. Or, pull out the rose design to use on a pillow or a pair of curtains. For additional tips and techniques, see the "Creative Stitching" sections of this book.

LACY LOOKS TO WEAR AND ENJOY

Lace Pattern Knitted Cardigan

Shown on pages 180–181.
Directions are for Size Medium (8–10); changes for Size Large (12–14) follow in parentheses. Bust = 36 (41) inches.

MATERIALS
Anny Blatt Ecoss'anny (50-gram balls): 17 (19) balls of ecru
Size 6 knitting needles, or size to obtain gauge given below
Size 6 circular knitting needle
Nine ⅜-inch-diameter buttons
Elastic thread for waistline

Abbreviations: Page 217.
Gauge: Over st st, 20 sts = 4 inches; 30 rows = 4 inches.

INSTRUCTIONS
The following stitch patterns are used to complete the sweater.

STOCKINETTE STITCH (st st): * K 1 row (right side); p 1 row (wrong side). Rep from * across.

REVERSE ST ST: * P 1 row (right side); k 1 row (wrong side). Rep from * across.

OPENWORK STITCH: Rep each row from * across. *Row 1:* * K 2 tog, yo. *Rows 2 and 4:* P across.
Row 3: * Yo, k 2 tog.

BOBBLE PAT: Rep each row from * across. *Row 1:* P across.
Row 2: K across.
Row 3: * P 3, **k in front, back, front, back, and front of next st—MB (make bobble) made;** p 8.
Row 4: * K 8, p 5, k 3. *Row 5:* * P 3, k 5, p 8. *Row 6:* * K 8, p 5 tog, k 3.
Row 7: * P 9, MB, p 2. *Row 8:* * K 2, p 5, k 9. *Row 9:* * P 9, k 5, p 2.
Row 10: * K 2, p 5 tog, k 9.
Rows 11–14: Rep Rows 3–6.
Row 15: P across. *Row 16:* K across.

DIAMOND PAT: Rep each row from * across. *Row 1:* * K 4, k 2 tog, yo, k 5. *Row 2 and all even-numbered rows:* P across.
Row 3: * K 3, k 2 tog, yo, k 1, yo, sl 1, k 1, psso, k 3. *Row 5:* * K 2, k 2 tog, yo, k 3, yo, sl 1, k 1, psso, k 2.
Row 7: * K 3, yo, sl 1, k 1, psso, k 1, k 2 tog, yo, k 3. *Row 9:* * K 4, yo, sl 1, k 2 tog, psso, yo, k 4.

LEAF PAT: Rep each row from * across. *Row 1:* P across.
Row 2: K across.
Row 3: * P 4, yo, k 1, yo, p 4.
Row 4: * K 4, p 3, k 4.
Row 5: * P 4, k 1, yo, k 1, yo, k 1, p 4. *Row 6:* * K 4, p 5, k 4.
Row 7: * P 4, k 2, yo, k 1, yo, k 2, p 4. *Row 8:* * K 4, p 7, k 4.
Row 9: * P 4, k 3, yo, k 1, yo, k 3, p 4. *Row 10:* * K 4, p 9, k 4.
Row 11: * P 4, sl 1, k 1, psso, k 5, k 2 tog, p 4. *Row 12:* * K 4, p 7, k 4.
Row 13: * P 4, sl 1, k 1, psso, k 3, k 2 tog, p 4. *Row 14:* * K 4, p 5, k 4.
Row 15: * P 4, sl 1, k 1, psso, k 1, k 2 tog, p 4. *Row 16:* * K 4, p 3, k 4.

CHART 1/LACE PATTERN KNITTED CARDIGAN

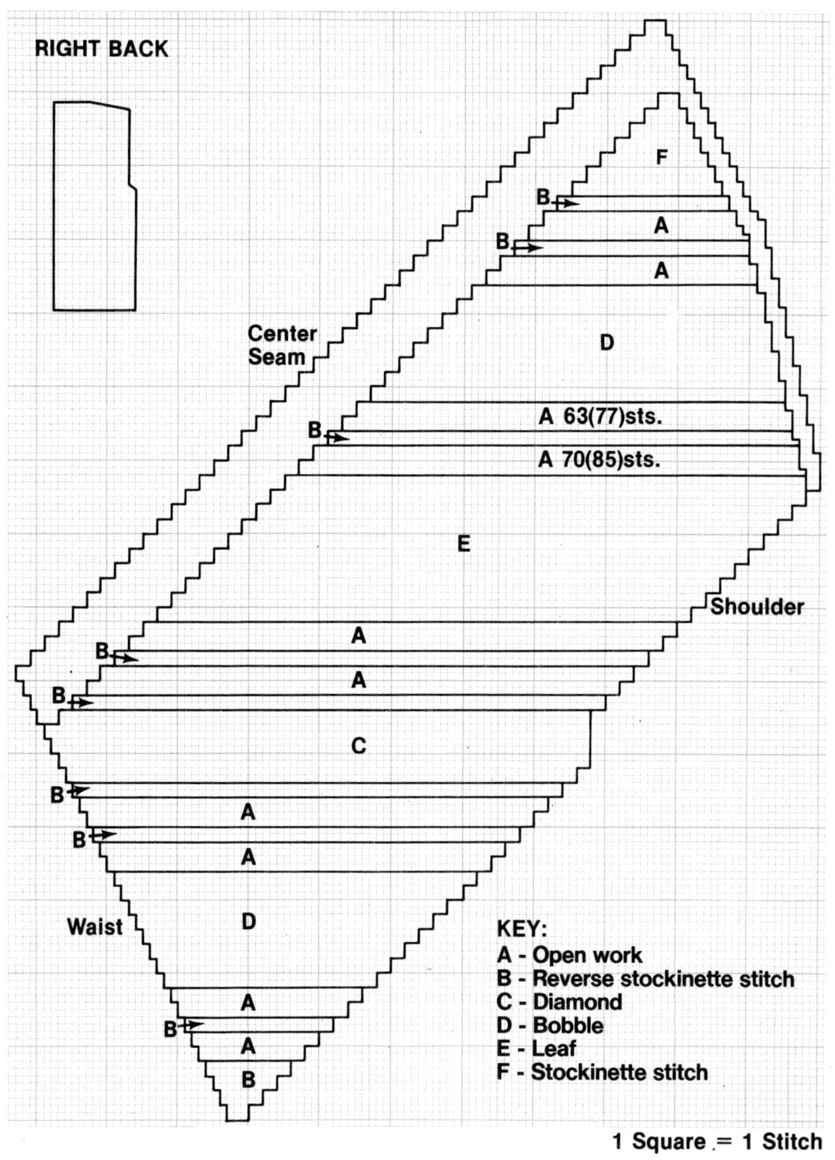

Row 17: * P 4, sl 1, k 2 tog, psso, p 4. *Row 18:* K across.

Row 19: P across. *Row 20:* K across.

BACK: Work Back in two halves, each knitted on the diagonal.

Note: To inc 1 st, k into front and back of st; to inc 2 sts, k into front, back, and front of st.

RIGHT BACK: Cast on 3 sts, work in reverse st st, then in pat sts, following Chart 1, *opposite,* and shaping as follows: At right edge, inc 2 sts every other row 24 times; work even (at right edge only) for 7 rows, then inc 2 sts every other row 15 (16) times. Dec 1 st every fourth row 9 times, every other row 9 (13) times. *At the same time,* at left edge, inc 1 st every other row 26 (30) times, then dec 2 sts every other row 43 (44) times. Bind off rem 3 sts.

For vertical placement of pattern stitches: Work pat sts bet shaping incs and decs at each edge, positioning extra stitches—those that are too few to make an additional pattern multiple—just inside the shaping at either or both edges. Work additional pattern multiples at either or both sides when sufficient incs permit and delete pattern multiples where decs encroach.

LEFT BACK: Work as for Right Back, reversing shapings.

LEFT FRONT: Cast on 3 sts, follow Chart 2, *right,* and work inc and dec as follows: At right, inc as for Right Back, then dec 1 st every fourth row 7 times. *At the same time,* at left, inc 1 st every other row 28 (30) times, then bind off 2 sts every other row 28 (29) times, then bind off 2 sts every other row 28 (29) times. Bind off rem 46 (48) sts. Work pat sts in same order as for Right Back, ending smaller size with second rep of Bobble Pat and ending larger size with 6 additional rows of reverse st st.

RIGHT FRONT: Work as for Left Front, reversing shapings.

CHART 2/LACE PATTERN KNITTED CARDIGAN

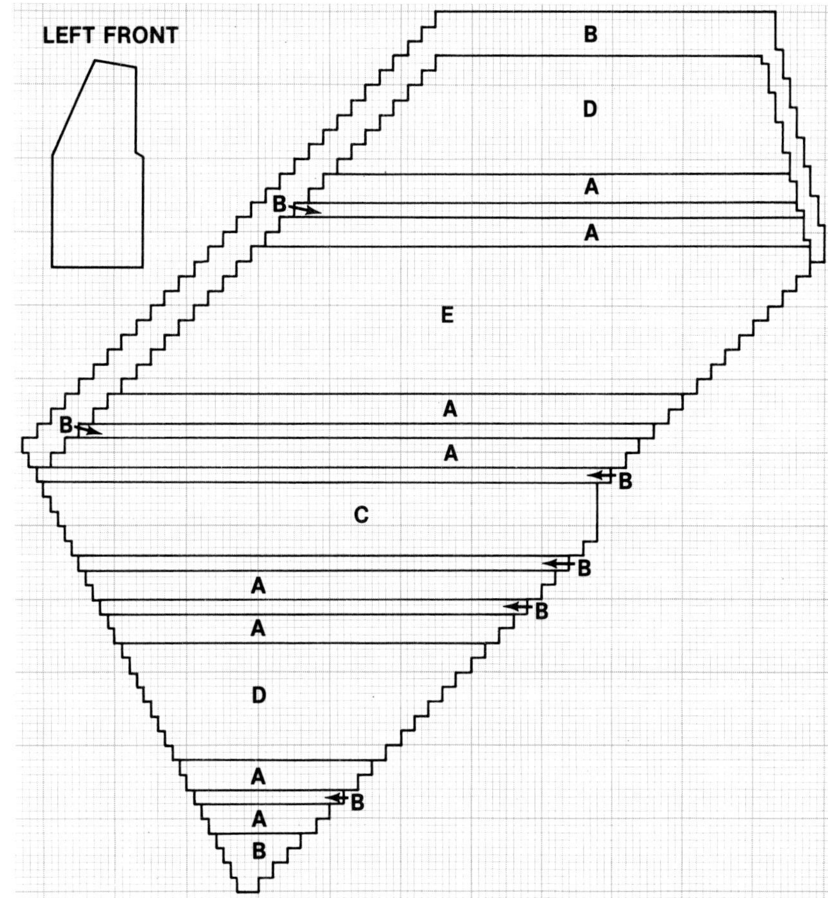

1 Square = 1 Stitch

SLEEVES (make 2): Cast on 50 (54) sts. Work in pat sts following Chart 3, page 190. Inc 1 st each side, alternating every 6th and 8th row 14 times—78 (82) sts. Work even to second rep of diamond pat.

TOP SHAPING: Bind off at each side every other row 3 sts once, 2 sts once, dec 1 st 19 times—30 (34) sts. *Next row:* (K 2 tog) across—15 (17) sts. Bind off rem sts.

FINISHING: Join two parts of Back, being careful to match pat rows. Join side seams similarly.

PEPLUM: *Note*—For Peplum and Front Borders, work all sl sts with yarn in back and sl as if to p. With right side facing and circular needle, pick up 189 (207) sts evenly spaced along bottom of sweater. Break off yarn and slide all sts to other end of needle.

Row 1: With right side facing and working in rows, and beg at same edge as for previous row, p 4, * sl 1, p 5; rep from * across, end sl 1, p 4.

Row 2 (wrong side): Work all sts as they appear; p the sl sts.

Row 3: Rep Row 1.

Row 4: Work sts as they appear; p the sl sts and inc 1 st each side of each sl st—251 (275) sts.

Row 5: P 5, * sl 1, p 7; rep from * across, ending with sl 1, p 5.

Row 6: Work sts as they appear; p the sl sts.

Row 7: Center a bobble motif in each p-7 grp as follows: P 5, * sl 1, p 3, MB, p 3; rep from * across, ending with sl 1, p 5.

Rows 8–9: Continue in bobble motif/sl st pat as established.

Row 10: Finish bobble motif, p the sl sts, *and at the same time* inc 1 st each side of each sl st—313 (343) sts.

continued

Row 11: P 6, * sl 1, p 9; rep from * across, end with sl 1, p 6.

Rows 12–14: Work in sl st pat as established. *Row 15:* Center a bobble motif in each p-9 grp as follows: P 6, * sl 1, p 4, MB, p 4; rep from * across, end with sl 1, p 6. *Rows 16–18:* Continue in sl st/bobble pat as established. *Rows 19–26:* Continue in sl st pat as established. *Row 27:* Bind off in sl st pat. Sew shoulders; match pat rows.

FRONT BORDERS: Work in two parts, then join at center back.

For Left Front Border: With right side facing and circular needle, pick up 155 (169) sts evenly spaced from middle of back neck to bottom of Peplum at left front. Break off yarn and slide all sts to other end of needle.

Row 1: With right side still facing, p 10, * sl 1, p 9; rep from * across, end with sl 1, p 4 (8). *Row 2:* Work all sts as they appear; p the sl sts. *Rows 3–4:* Rep Rows 1–2.

Row 5: Center 1 bobble motif in each p-9 grp as follows: P 5, MB, p 4, * sl 1, p 4, MB, p 4; rep from * across, end with sl 1, p 4 (8).

Rows 6–8: Continue in sl st/bobble pat as established.

Rows 9–13: Work sl st pat as established. *Row 14:* Bind off in pat.

For Right Front Border: With right side facing and circular needle, pick up 155 (169) sts evenly spaced from bottom of peplum at right front to middle of back neck; break off yarn and slide all sts to other end of needle.

Work as for Left Front Border, reversing placement on Row 1 as follows: P 4 (8), * sl 1, p 9; rep from * across, end with sl 1, p 10.

Rows 2–4: Work sl st pat as established. *Row 5:* Center buttonhole in each of first nine p-9 grps (beg at lower edge of sweater) as follows: P 4 (8), * sl 1, p 3, bind off 3 sts, p 3; rep from * 8 times more; continue in sl st pat, centering bobble in each of rem p-9 grps. *Row 6:* Continue in bobble pat, cast on 3 sts above bind-off sts of Row 5.

Rows 7–8: Continue in sl st pat over buttonholes, continue in bobble pat in rem p-9 grps. *Rows 9–13:* Continue in sl st pat. *Row 14:* Bind off in pat.

CUFFS: With right side facing and circular needle, pick up 49 (53) sts evenly spaced along bottom of each sleeve; break off yarn and slide all sts to other end of needle. Work as for Peplum as follows: *Row 1:* With right side still facing, and beg at same edge as previous row, p 3 (5), * sl 1, p 5; rep from * across, end sl 1, p 3 (5). *Row 2:* Work sts as they appear; p the sl sts.

Row 3: Continue in sl st pat as established, inc 1 st each side of each sl st—65 (69) sts. *Row 4:* Continue in sl st pat. *Row 5:* Center 1 bobble in each p-7 grp as follows: P 4 (6), * sl 1, p 3, MB, p 3; rep from * across, end sl 1, p 4 (6).

CHART 3/LACE PATTERN KNITTED CARDIGAN

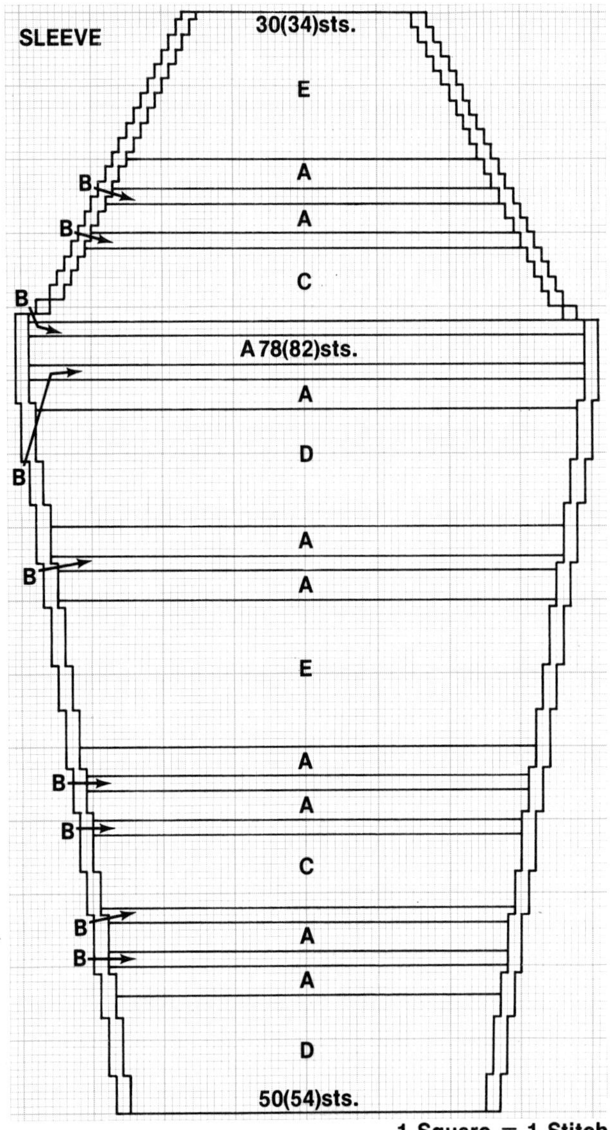

1 Square = 1 Stitch

Rows 6–8: Continue in sl st/bobble pat as established.

Row 9: Continue in sl st pat, inc 1 st each side of each sl st—81 (85) sts. *Rows 10–12:* Continue in sl st pat as established.

Row 13: Center 1 bobble motif in each p-9 grp as follows: P 5 (7), * sl 1, p 4, MB, p 4; rep from * across, end with sl 1, p 5 (7).

Rows 14–16: Continue in sl st/bobble pat as established.

Rows 17–20: Continue in sl st pat as established.

Row 21: Bind off in pat.

Seam sleeve and cuff; set in sleeves. Seam center back of border. Insert buttons in 9 bobbles opposite buttonholes and close on wrong side with invisible sts. Insert two strands of elastic through seam at top of Peplum; gather to fit.

Crocheted V-Neck Collar

Shown on page 182.

MATERIALS

J. & P. Coats Knit-Cro-Sheen Mercerized Cotton (350-yard ball): 1 ball of No. 1 white

Size 7 steel crochet hook

Abbreviations: Page 211.

Gauge: 4 dc and 3 ch-1s to make 3 meshes as for Row 1 = 1 inch.

INSTRUCTIONS

Beg at inner edge of collar, ch 200 having 9 ch sts = 1 inch.

Row 1 (right side): Dc in sixth ch from hook to form first sp; mark this sp to be used later; (ch 1, sk next ch, dc in next ch) 47 times; ch 1, sk next ch; in next ch make (dc, ch 1) twice *and* dc; (ch 1, sk next ch, dc in next ch) 49 times—100 ch-1 sps; ch 4, turn.

Row 2: Sk first dc, (dc in next dc, ch 1) 48 times; in next dc make dc, ch 1 and dc; in next dc make (dc, ch 1) twice *and* dc; in next dc make dc, ch 1 and dc; (ch 1, dc in next dc) 48 times; ch 1, sk next ch of turning ch, dc in next ch; ch 4, turn.

Row 3: Sk first dc, (dc in next dc, ch 1) 48 times; in next dc make dc, ch 1 and dc; ch 1, sk next dc, (in next dc make dc, ch 1 and dc; ch 1) 3 times; sk next dc; in next dc make dc, ch 1 and dc; (ch 1, dc in next dc) 48 times; ch 1, dc in third ch of turning ch-4. Ch 4, turn.

Row 4: In first ch-1 sp make **trc, ch 1 and 2 trc—beg 4-trc shell made;** ch 2, (sk next sp; in next sp make **2 trc, ch 1 and 2 trc—4-trc shell made,** ch 2) twice; * sk 1 sp, (4-trc shell in next sp, ch 2) 3 times; (sk 1 sp, 4-trc shell in next sp, ch 2) 3 times. Rep from * 3 times; sk 1 sp, (4-trc shell in next sp, ch 2) 3 times; (4-trc shell in next ch-1 sp, ch 2) 11 times; ** (sk 1 sp, 4-trc shell in next sp, ch 2) 3 times; sk 1 sp, (4-trc shell in next sp, ch 2) 3 times. Rep from ** to last 6 sps, (sk 1 sp, 4-trc shell in next sp, ch 2) twice; sk 1 sp; in last sp **make 2 trc, ch 1 and trc; trc in top of ch-4—end 4-trc shell made**—65 shells; ch 4, turn.

Rows 5–6: Make starting 4-trc shell in ch-1 sp of first shell; * ch 2; **4-trc shell in ch-1 sp of next shell—shell over shell made.** Rep from * to last shell, ch 2, make end-trc shell over last shell and ch-4; ch 4, turn.

Row 7: In sp of first shell **make 2 trc, ch 2 and 3 trc—starting 6-trc shell made;** (ch 2; in sp of next shell **make 3 trc, ch 2 and 3 trc—6-trc shell made**) 15 times; (ch 2, 6-dtr shell over shell) 33 times; (ch 2, 6-trc shell over shell) 15 times; ch 2; **make 3 trc, ch 2 and 2 trc in last sp, trc in top of ch-4—end 6-trc shell made;** ch 4, turn.

Row 8: Starting 6-trc shell over first shell, (ch 2, 6-trc shell over shell) 15 times; (ch 2, 6-dtr shell over shell, ch 2, dtr in next ch-2 sp) 32 times; ch 2, 6-dtr shell over shell, (ch 2, 6-trc shell over shell) 15 times; ch 2, end 6-trc shell over last shell and ch-4; fasten off, turn.

Row 9: Join thread to ch-2 sp between thirteenth and fourteenth shell; (ch 2, 6-trc shell over next shell) 3 times; (ch 2, 6-dtr shell over shell, ch 2, sk next ch-2 sp, dtr in dtr between shells) 32 times; ch 2, 6-dtr shell over shell, (ch 2, 6-trc shell over shell) 3 times; ch 2, sl st in next ch-2 sp between shells; do not work over rem sts; fasten off, turn.

Row 10: Sk first 2 shells, join thread to next ch-2 sp, ch 2, 6-trc shell over shell, (ch 2, 6-dtr shell over next shell, ch 2, sk next ch-2 sp, dtr in next dtr) 32 times; ch 2, 6-dtr shell over shell, ch 2, 6-trc shell over shell, ch 2, sl st in next sp; do not work over rem sts; fasten off, turn. *Row 11:* Sk first 2 shells and next ch-2 sp, join thread to next dtr, (ch 2, 6-dtr shell over shell, ch 2, sk next ch-2 sp, dtr in next dtr) 30 times; ch 2, 6-dtr shell over shell, ch 2, sk next ch-2 sp, sl st in next dtr; do not work over rem sts; fasten off, turn.

Row 12: Sk first 2 shells and next ch-2 sp, join thread to next dtr, (ch 2, 6-dtr shell over shell, ch 2, sk next ch-2 sp, dtr in next dtr) 26 times; ch 2, 6-dtr shell over shell, ch 2, sk next ch-2 sp, sl st in next dtr; do not work over rem sts; fasten off, turn.

Row 13: Sk first 2 shells and next ch-2 sp, join thread to next dtr, (ch 2, 6-dtr shell over shell, ch 2, sk next ch-2 sp, dtr in next dtr) 22 times; ch 2, 6-dtr shell over shell, ch 2, sk next ch-2 sp, sl st in next dtr; do not work over rem sts; fasten off, turn.

EDGING: Join thread to marked sp, * ch 5, sc in end st of next row. Rep from * to next corner. Work along outer edge as follows: ** **Ch 3, holding back on hook last lp of each dc, make 2 dc in last sc, thread over and draw through all lps on hook—cluster made;** (ch 3, make a cluster in tip of previous cluster) twice; sk next shell, sc in next sp. Rep from ** to opposite corner; ch 5 and work along next narrow edge to correspond with other narrow edge; fasten off.

To adjust inner edge of collar make a chain of desired length; leave a tail at both ends. Weave chain through sps of Row 1, adjust and secure.

Crocheted Dress

Shown on page 183.
Directions are for Size Small (8–10); changes for Size Large (12–14) follow in parentheses. Bust = 31½–32½ (34–36) inches. Hips = 31–33 (34–36) inches.

MATERIALS
Coats & Clark Royal Mouliné Knit and Crochet Thread: 15 (16) balls No. 001 white
Size 4 steel crochet hook
1 yard of elastic

Abbreviations: Page 211.
Gauge: Excluding picots, diameters of motifs are as follows: Motif A—3 inches; B—2¾ inches; C—2½ inches; D—2¼ inches; E—2 inches; F—1¾ inches.

INSTRUCTIONS
MOTIF A: Ch 5; join with sl st to form ring. *Rnd 1:* Ch 1, make 12 sc in ring; join with sl st to first sc.

Rnd 2: Ch 4, * dc in next sc, ch 1; rep from * around; join to third ch of ch-4 at beg of rnd—12 ch-1 sps.

Rnd 3: Ch 1, sc in joining, * ch 4, sc in next dc; rep from * around, end ch 2, hdc in first sc to form last lp—12 ch-4 lps. *Rnd 4:* Ch 1, sc in lp just made, ch 5, * sc in next lp, ch 5; rep from * around; join to first sc.

Rnds 5–6: Ch 1, sc in joining, ch 6, * sc in next sc, ch 6; rep from * around; join to first sc.

Rnds 7–8: Ch 1, sc in joining, ch 7, * sc in next sc, ch 7; rep from * around; join as before. *Rnd 9:* Ch 1, sc in joining, ch 8, * sc in next sc, ch 8; rep from * around; join.

Rnd 10: Ch 1, **in join make sc, ch 5, and sc—beg picot made;** (ch 8, sc in next sc, ch 8, **in next sc make sc, ch 5, sc—picot made**) 5 times; ch 8, sc in next sc, ch 8; join to first sc; fasten off.

MOTIF B: Work as for Motif A through Rnd 7. *Rnd 8:* Ch 1, make beg picot in joining, (ch 7, sc in next sc, ch 7, picot in next sc) 5 times; ch 7, sc in next sc, ch 7; join to first sc; fasten off.

HALF-MOTIF B: Work as for Motif A through Rnd 1. *Row 1:* Ch 4, dc in next sc, (ch 1, dc in next sc) 6 times; do not work over rem sts; ch 1, *turn. Row 2:* Sc in first dc, (ch 4, sc in next dc) 6 times; ch 2, hdc in third ch of ch-4 to form last lp; ch 1, *turn. Row 3:* Sc in lp just formed, (ch 4, sc in next lp) 6 times; ch 1, *turn. Row 4:* Sc in first sc, (ch 5, sc in next sc) 6 times; ch 1, *turn.*

Rows 5–6: Sc in first sc, (ch 6, sc in next sc) 6 times; ch 1, *turn.*

Row 7: Make picot in first sc, (ch 7, sc in next sc, ch 7, picot in next sc) 3 times; fasten off.

MOTIF C: Work as for Motif A through Rnd 6. *Rnd 7:* Ch 1, make beg picot in joining, (ch 6, sc in next sc, ch 6, picot in next sc) 5 times; ch 6, sc in next sc, ch 6, join; fasten off.

HALF-MOTIF C: Work as for Half-Motif B through Row 5. *Row 6:* Work as for Row 7 of Half-Motif B making ch-6 instead of ch-7.

MOTIF D: Work as for Motif A through Rnd 5. *Rnd 6:* Ch 1, make beg picot in joining, (ch 6, sc in next sc, ch 6, picot in next sc) 5 times; ch 6, sc in next sc, ch 6, join; fasten off.

HALF-MOTIF D: Work as for Half-Motif B through Row 4. *Row 5:* Work as for Row 7 of Half-Motif B, making ch-6 instead of ch-7.

MOTIF E: Work as for Motif A through Rnd 4. *Rnd 5:* Ch 1, make beg picot in joining, (ch 5, sc in next sc, ch 5, picot in next sc) 5 times; ch 7, sc in next sc, ch 7, join; fasten off.

HALF-MOTIF E: Work as for Half-Motif B through Row 3. *Row 4:* Work as for Row 7 of Half-Motif B; make ch-5 instead of ch-7.

MOTIF F: Work as for Motif A through Rnd 3. *Rnd 4:* Ch 1, sc in lp just formed, (ch 4, picot in next lp, ch 4, sc in next lp) 5 times; ch 4, picot in next lp, ch 4, join; fasten off.

HALF-MOTIF F: Work as for Motif A through Rnd 1. *Rows 1–2:* Rep Rows 1-2 of Half-Motif B; ch 1, *turn. Row 3:* Make picot in first lp, (ch 4, sc in next lp, ch 4, picot in next lp) 3 times; fasten off.

SKIRT: *For Size Small*—make motifs as follows: 84 B, 84 C, 42 D, 21 E, 63 F. *For Size Large*—make motifs as follows: 84 A, 84 B, 42 C, 21 D, 21 E, and 42 F. Following chart, *opposite,* sew motifs tog joining picots to corresponding picots and scs to corresponding scs. Sew back seam.

TOP EDGING: Join thread to a free picot at top edge.

Rnd 1: Ch 1, sc in same place, * ch 3, trc in next lp, ch 1, trc in joining bet motifs, ch 1, trc in next lp, ch 3, sc in next picot; rep from * around, end with ch 3; join to first sc.

Rnd 2: Working over elastic, ch 1, sc evenly around; join, fasten off. Adjust elastic to fit and secure ends.

TOP—BACK AND FRONT: *For Size Small*—make 98 Motifs C and 8 Half-Motifs C. *For Size Large*—make 98 Motifs B and 8 Half-Motifs B. Following chart, *opposite,* place 2 markers where indicated by dots. Sew motifs tog same as for Skirt. Sew side seam, then sew the 5-motif edge in place bet markers.

SLEEVE (make 2): *For Size Small*—make 11 Motifs D, 8 Motifs E, 5 Motifs F, 2 Half-Motifs E and 2 Half-Motifs F. *For Size Large*—make 11 Motifs C, 8 Motifs D, 5 Motifs E, 2 Half-Motifs D and 2 Half-Motifs E. Following chart for Sleeve, *opposite,* sew motifs tog. Sew in sleeves, easing to fit.

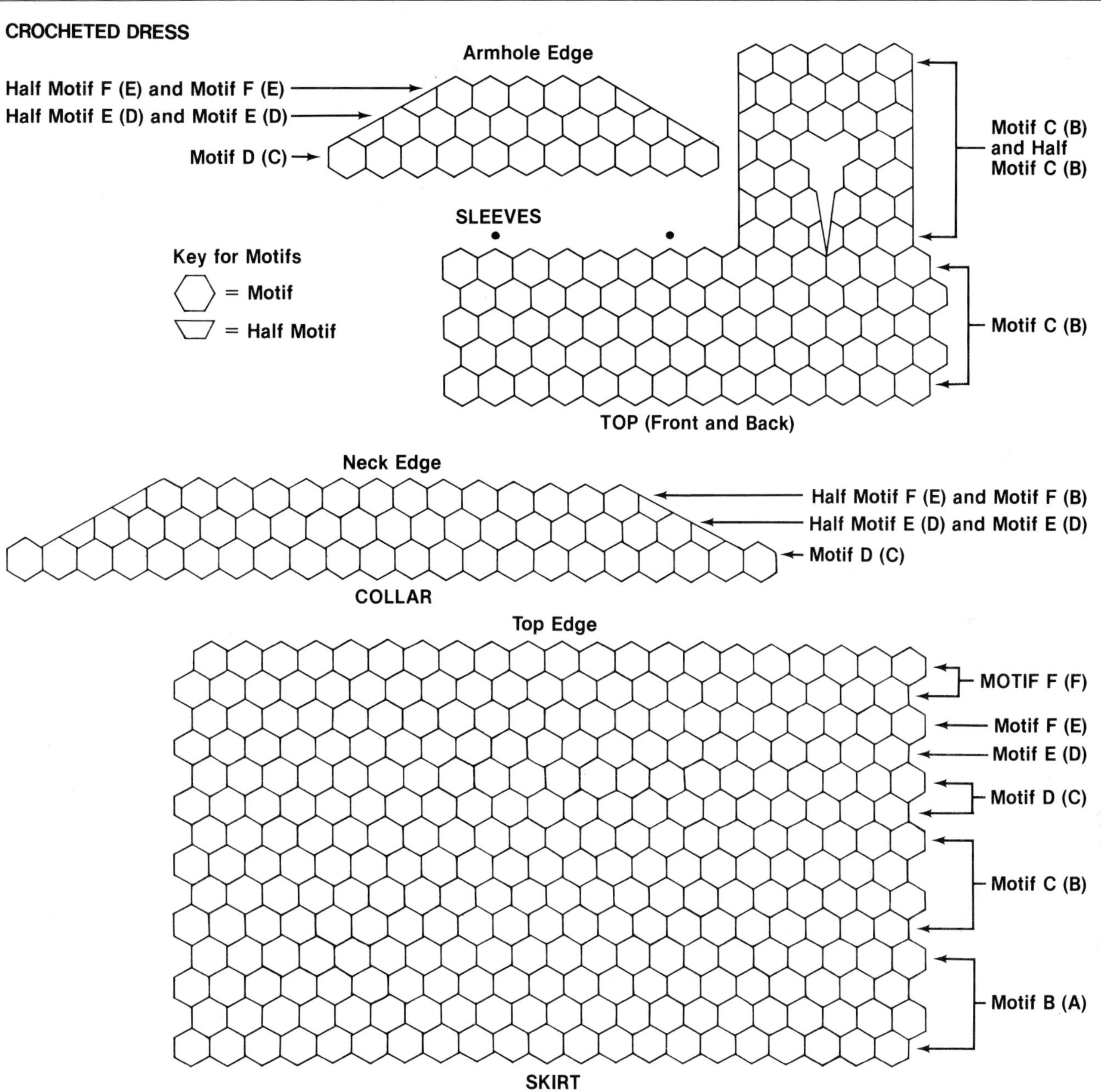

COLLAR: *For Size Small*—make 22 Motifs D, 17 Motifs E, 14 Motifs F, and 2 Half-Motifs F. *For Size Large*—make 22 Motifs C, 17 Motifs D, 14 Motifs E, and 2 Half-Motifs E. Following chart, *above*, sew motifs tog. Gather collar neckline to fit neck opening and sew into place.

TIE: Make a 50-inch-long ch; sl st in second ch from hook and in each ch across; fasten off. Beg at center front, lace tie through free picot of each motif along lower edge.

Antique Gloves

Shown on page 184.

MATERIALS

Clark's Big Ball 3-Cord Crochet Cotton, Size 30: 2 balls of No. 1 White

Size 12 steel crochet hook

Abbreviations: Page 211.

INSTRUCTIONS

GLOVE (make 2): Starting at wrist, ch 100 to measure about 8½ inches. Being careful not to twist chain, join with sl st to first sc.

Rnd 1: Ch 1, sc in joining, * **ch 4, sl st in fourth ch from hook—picot made,** ch 3, sk next 3 ch, sc in next ch; rep from * around to last 3 ch on ring, ch 4, sl st in fourth ch from hook, dc in first sc to form last lp—25 picot-lps.

Rnd 2: Ch 1, sc in lp just formed, * make picot, ch 3, sc in the ch following the picot on next lp; rep from * around, end with picot, dc in first sc. Rep Rnd 2 for pat; work until total length is 3½ inches.

continued

THUMB OPENING: *Rnd 1:* Ch 1, sc in lp just formed; ch 8, sk next 5 lps for Thumb Opening, sc in next picot-lp as before; complete row in picot-lp pat; end as for Rnd 2 above.

Rnd 2: Ch 1, sc in lp just made, make picot, ch 3, sk first ch on ch-8 lp, sc in next ch, (make picot, ch 3, sk next 2 ch on ch-8 lp, sc in next ch) twice; sk last ch on ch-8 lp, make picot, ch 3, sc in next lp; complete row in picot-lp pat, ending as before.

Continue in picot-lp pat until glove when tried on reaches index finger; fasten off at end of last rnd. Put on glove; with 6 small safety pins mark lps for position of fingers on palm and back.

INDEX FINGER: *Rnd 1:* Attach thread to marked lp on back between index and middle fingers, ch 1, sc in same lp, ch 8, sc in corresponding marked lp on palm, * ch 5, sc in next lp on index finger. Rep from * to ch-8 lp; (ch 5, sk next 2 ch, sc in next ch) twice; ch 2, dc in first sc to form last lp.

Rnd 2: Ch 1, sc in lp just formed, * ch 5, sc in next lp; rep from * around; end ch 2, dc in first sc. Rep last rnd until work is ¼ inch shorter than length of finger.

Last Rnd: Ch 3, dc in each lp around; join to top of ch-3. Break off; draw sts of last rnd tog; secure.

MIDDLE FINGER: *Rnd 1:* Attach thread to marked lp on back between middle and ring fingers, ch 1, sc in same lp, ch 8, sc in corresponding lp on palm, then work ch-5 lps to next ch-8 lp; (ch 5, sk 2 ch on ch-8 lp, sc in next ch) twice; ch 5, sk last 2 ch of same ch-8 lp, sc in next lp, work ch-5 lps, end with ch 2, dc in first sc, (ch 5, sk next 2 ch on ch-8, sc in ch) twice; ch 5, sc in next lp; work rem finger as for previous finger.

RING FINGER: Work same as for Middle Finger.

LITTLE FINGER: Attach thread to lp following ch-8 lp of ring finger. *Rnd 1:* Ch 1, sc in same lp, make ch-5 lps to next ch-8 lp of ring finger, sc in next ch; (ch 5, sk 2 ch, sc in next ch) twice; ch 2, dc in first sc; complete finger in same manner as other fingers.

THUMB: Attach thread to lp following the ch-8 lp. *Rnd 1:* Ch 1, sc in same lp, make ch-5 lps to next ch-8 lp, ch 5, sk next ch on ch-8, sc in next ch, (ch 5, sk next 2 ch, sc in next ch) twice; ch 2, dc in first sc. Complete as for Index Finger.

CUFF: Working along opposite side of starting chain, attach thread to any ch of starting chain.

Rnd 1: Ch 2, sk next ch, hdc in next ch and in each ch st around. Join to top of ch-2.

Rnd 2: Ch 1, sc in joining, * ch 4, sk next 2 sts, sc in next st; rep from * around to last 2 ch; ch 2, hdc in first sc to form last lp.

Rnds 3–5: Ch 1, sc in lp just formed, * ch 4, sc in next lp; rep from * around, end with ch 2, hdc in first sc. *Rnd 6:* Ch 4, * hdc in next lp, ch 2; rep from * around; join last ch-2 to second ch of ch-4.

Rnd 7: Ch 1, sc in joining, 3 sc in next sp, * sc in next hdc, 3 sc in next sp; rep from * around; join to first sc.

EDGING: Ch 1, sc in joining, [(ch 4, sk next 3 sc, sc in next sc) twice; ch 1, *turn;* make 7 sc in each of 2 lps just made, sl st in sc of last lp; ch 1, *turn,* sl st in next 3 sc, sc in next sc, ch 4, sc in center sc of next lp; ch 1, *turn;* 3 sc, ch 3, 3 sc in last lp, sl st in next sc; fasten off.]

* With right side facing, sk next 3 sc on Rnd 7, attach thread to next sc, ch 1, sc in same place; rep bet [ ]s. Rep from * around.

ROSE (make 6): Beg at center, ch 5. Join with sl st to form ring.

Rnd 1: Ch 5, (dc in ring, ch 2) 4 times; join to third ch of ch-5.

Rnd 2: Ch 1, in *each* ch-2 lp around make petals of sc, hdc, 3 dc, hdc and sc; join to first sc.

Rnd 3: * Ch 4, holding petal forward, sc in sc bet next 2 petals of previous rnd; rep from * around; join with sl st in first ch of ch-4 lp.

Rnd 4: Ch 1; in *each* ch-4 lp around make sc, hdc, 5 dc, hdc and sc; fasten off.

DISC (make 4): Ch 6, sl st in first ch to form ring. *Rnd 1:* Ch 3, make 15 dc in ring; join to top of ch-3.

Rnd 2: Ch 1, sc in joining and each dc; join to first sc; fasten off.

LEAF (make 2): Ch 2, sc in second ch from hook, (ch 5, sl st in last sc made) 3 times; make 10 sc in *each* ch-5 lp; join to first sc; fasten off. Tack roses, discs, and leaf at random to back of glove.

Crocheted Collar

Shown on page 185.

MATERIALS

½ yard of light blue broadcloth for backing the lace while working
Thread; pins, thumbtacks; embroidery needles
Clark's Big Ball 3-Cord Crochet Cotton, Size 10: 1 ball of white; Size 30: 1 ball of white
Clark's "Tatting-Crochet" Cotton, Size 70: 2 balls of white
Sizes 10 and 13 steel crochet hooks; two pairs of 16-inch-long artist stretcher strips

Abbreviations: Page 211.

INSTRUCTIONS

In the directions that follow, PC = padding cord; pc = picot.

Cut two 18-inch squares of blue fabric; set one aside. Trace pattern, page 195, onto remaining square, joining pieces at A–B and flopping

continued

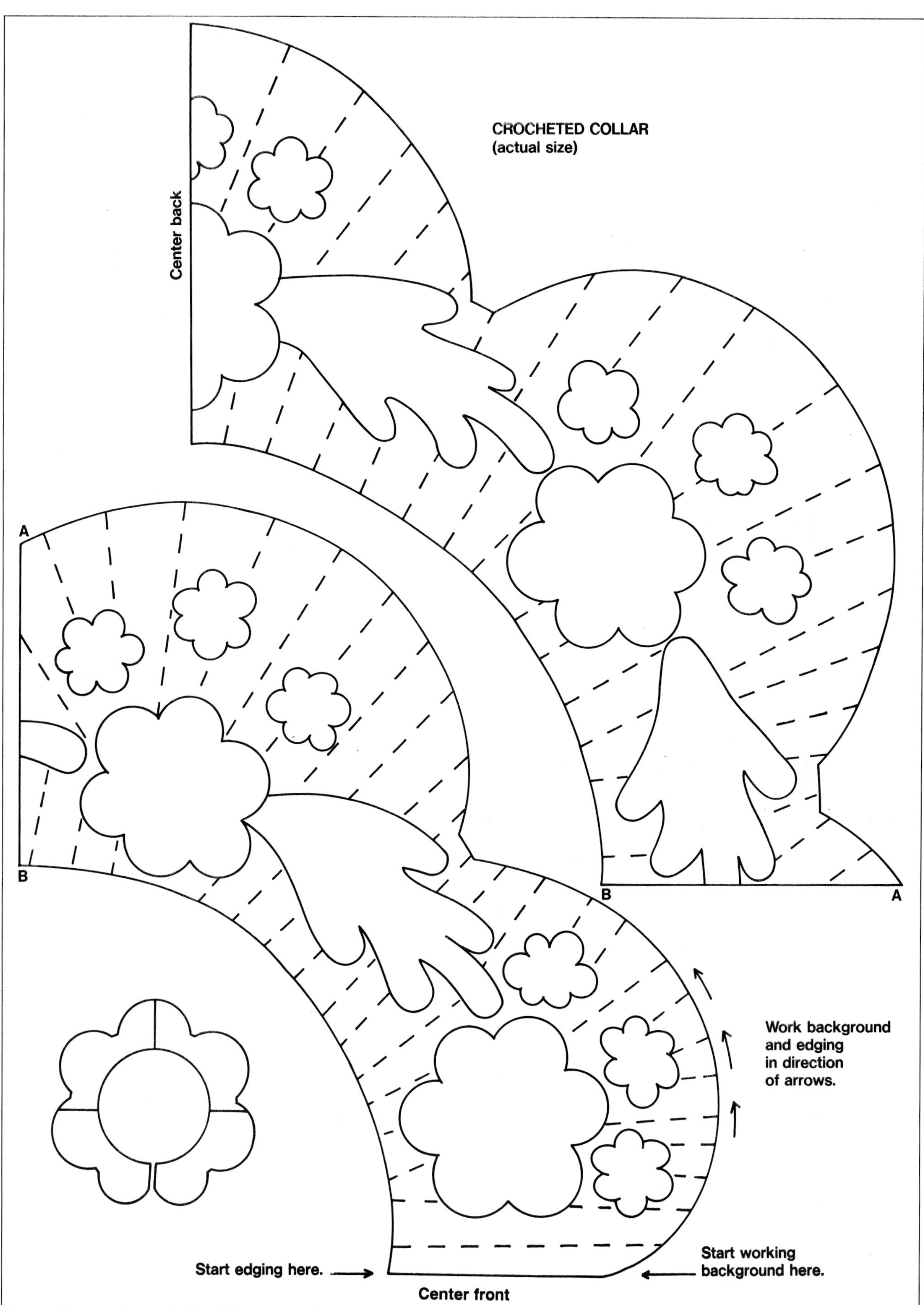
CROCHETED COLLAR
(actual size)
Center back
A
B
B
A
Work background
and edging
in direction
of arrows.
Start edging here.
Start working
background here.
Center front

pattern along center to complete. Pin fabric atop first blue square. Hem squares together, stretch over assembled stretcher strips, and tack into place. Set aside.

ROSE (make 7): With Size 10 hook and Size 30 thread, ch 8, sl st to form ring. *Rnd 1:* Ch 5, dc in ring, (ch 3, dc in ring) 4 times, ch 3, sl st third ch of beg ch-5—6 ch-3 lps.

Rnd 2: In *each* ch-3 lp work (sc, hdc, 3 dc, hdc, sc—petal made); join with sl st to first sc.

Rnd 3: * Ch 5, holding petal forward, sl st bet next 2 petals; rep from * around; do not join. *Rnd 4:* In *each* ch-5 lp work (sc, hdc, 5 dc, hdc, sc); join to first sc.

Rnd 5: * Ch 7, holding petal forward, sl st bet next 2 petals; rep from * around; do not join.

Rnd 6: In *each* ch-7 lp work (sc, hdc, 7 dc, hdc, sc); join to first sc; fasten off.

LEAF (make 6): With Size 10 hook, Size 30 thread as working thread, and Size 10 thread as PC, work 18 sc over PC, ch 1, turn.

Row 2: Make 12 sc over PC and into previous sc—6 sts rem; ch 1, turn. *Row 3:* 8 sc into PC and previous sc—4 sts free. Work 10 sc over PC alone, ch 1, turn.

Row 4: Rep Row 2. *Row 5:* Rep Row 3. *Row 6:* 18 sc over PC and into previous sts, ch 1, turn.

Row 7: 8 sc over PC and into previous sts—10 sts free; 4 sc over PC alone, ch 1, turn.

Row 8: 12 sc over PC and into previous sts, 6 sc over PC alone, sl st to first st from Row 3, ch 1, turn.

Row 9: 8 sc over PC and into previous sts, 4 sc over PC alone, ch 1, turn. *Row 10:* 12 sc over PC and into previous sts, 6 sc over PC alone, sl st to beginning. 13 sc over PC alone, ch 1, turn.

Row 11: 12 sc over PC and into previous sts, sl st over PC and into 13th sc, ch 1, turn. *Row 12:* 13 sc over PC and into previous sts. Fasten off leaving long threads. Fold over bottom part of leaf; cover the two open triangles. Sew in place; tie in thread ends.

FLOWERET (make 21): With Size 10 hook and Size 30 thread, ch 8, join with sl st to form ring.

Rnd 1: Ch 3, (sc in ring, ch 2) 5 times, sl st to first ch of ch-3 lp—6 lps. *Rnd 2:* Into *each* lp around, work (sl st, 3 dc, sl st); fasten off.

BACKGROUND: Tie in ends and block motifs; baste to blue background fabric. With Size 70 thread and Size 13 hook, work in direction of dotted lines on pattern.

Row 1: Over a 6-inch length of ch, **sc in fourth ch from hook—picot (pc) made;** ch 5, sk 4 ch, sl st in next ch, * ch 6, make pc, ch 5, sk 4 ch, sl st in next ch, rep from * across, end with ch 6, pc, ch 2, dc in last base ch.

Row 2: Ch 9, sl st into next sp; * ch 6, pc, ch 5, sl st in next sp, rep from * across, end with ch 6, pc, ch 2, dc in last sp.

Rep Rows 1 and 2 for pat.

Because work is sewn to fabric, at end of row *rotate frame* to crochet into previous row. To adapt picot pattern, make it smaller in tight areas and larger in wider areas. Work up to motif, join, rotate work; continue crocheting in direction of dotted lines. Pin or tack background mesh to collar edges to obtain correct shaping. Whipstitch motifs together with thread in places where motifs should touch but are not connected.

EDGING: Cut basting threads; remove collar from background. Use Size 30 thread for working thread, Size 10 for PC, and Size 10 hook.

Rnd 1: Beg at inner edge of left back (marked on pattern), sc over PC and over lps of background crochet around collar, following pattern outline. Sl st to first sc.

Rnd 2: Ch 1, 2 sc in same st as join; * ch 5, sk 4 sc, 3 sc in next st, rep from * around *outside edge* of collar. For *neck edge* work as follows: * Ch 3, sk 2 sts, sc in next st, ch 3, sk 1 st, sc in next st; rep from * to end, sl st to first sc.

Rnd 3: Ch 6, * trc in third ch of ch-5 lp, **ch 5, sc in second ch from hook—picot made,** ch 1, trc in same ch, make picot, (ch 3, sc in same ch) twice, ch 2, trc in same ch; ch 3, sc in third ch of next ch-5 lp, ch 3, rep from * until beg of neck edge; fasten off. Pull PC to adjust tension; finish ends and block.

Crocheted Stole

Shown on page 186.
Finished size is 17x64 inches, excluding eyelet trim.

MATERIALS

J. & P. Coats Knit-Cro-Sheen (250-yard balls): 8 balls of white
Size 8 steel crochet hook
3 yards of 2½-inch-wide pregathered eyelet edging

Abbreviations: Page 211.

INSTRUCTIONS

FIRST MOTIF: Beg at center, ch 10; join with sl st to form ring.

Rnd 1: Ch 1, make 16 sc in ring; join with sl st to first sc.

Rnd 2: Ch 8, * sk next sc, dc in next sc, ch 5; rep from * around; join to third ch of beg ch-8—8 sps made. *Rnd 3:* * Ch 1, in next ch-5 lp make sc, hdc, 3 dc, hdc and sc; rep from * around; join to first ch-1.

Rnd 4: Ch 9, sc in center dc of petal, * ch 5, sk next 7 sts, sc in following dc; **ch 5, in next ch-1 sp make trc, ch 5, sk 3 sts, sc in following dc—corner made.** Rep from * 2 more times, ch 5, sk 7 sts, sc in following dc, ch 5, join with sl st in fourth ch of ch-9.

Rnd 5: Ch 3, dc in same place as join; (make 5 dc in next sp) 3 times; * 3 dc in corner trc, (make 5 dc in next sp) 3 times; rep from * around, dc in same ch as beg ch-3; join to top of ch-3. *Rnd 6:* Sl st in next dc, (ch 5, sk 3 dc, sc in following dc) 4 times; * **ch 7, sk next dc, sc in next dc—corner lp made;** (ch 5, sk 3 dc, sc in following dc) 4 times; rep from * around; end ch 7, join to first sl st; fasten off.

SECOND MOTIF: *Rnds 1-5:* Work same as First Motif.

Rnd 6: Sl st in next dc, (ch 5, sk 3 dc, sc in next dc) 4 times; ch 3, sl st in fourth ch of ch-7 corner lp of First Motif; ch 3, sk next dc on Second Motif, sc in next dc, (ch 2, sl st in third ch of next ch-5 lp of First Motif, ch 2, sk 3 dc on Second Motif, sc in next dc) 4 times; ch 3, sl st in fourth ch of corner lp of First Motif, ch 3, sk next dc on Second Motif, sc in next dc. Complete as for First Motif. Fasten off.

Make 23 rows of 6 motifs, joining adjacent sides as Second Motif was joined to First Motif. Where corners meet, join third and fourth corners to joining of previous two corners.

EDGING: Attach thread to fourth ch of any free corner lp, ch 1, sc in same ch, (ch 5, sc in third ch of next ch-5 lp) 4 times; * ch 5, sc in next joining motifs; (ch 5, sc in third ch of next ch-5 lp) 4 times; rep from * to next corner; ch 5, sc in fourth ch of ch-7 lp, (ch 5, sc in third ch of next ch-5 lp) 4 times **; rep from first * to ** around; end ch 5, join to first sc; fasten off. Sew on eyelet.

Filet Jacket

Shown on page 187.
Directions are for Small (10-12); changes for Medium are in parentheses.

MATERIALS
Bucilla Tempo (2-ounce skeins): 14 (15) skeins
Size 1 steel crochet hook

Abbreviations: Page 211.
Gauge: 2 mesh and 3 dc = 1 inch.

INSTRUCTIONS

BACK—BORDER: Ch 120 (126) for lower edge. *Row 1* (right side): Dc in fourth ch from hook and in each rem ch—118 (124) sts.

Row 2: Ch 1, turn, work 1 sc in each dc to end and top of turning ch. *Row 3:* Ch 3, turn, work 1 dc in second sc and in each sc to end.

Row 4: Rep Row 2.

BACK—MESH PAT: *Row 1:* Ch 5, turn, * sk 2 sts, dc in next st, ch 2; rep from * across, end dc in last st—39 (41) mesh. *Row 2:* Ch 5, turn, dc in second dc, * ch 2, dc in next dc; rep from * across, end ch 2, dc in third ch of turning ch-5. Rep Row 2 for pat until 20 inches from beg, or desired length to underarm. Mark for underarm. Work in pat until 7 (7½) inches from marker; fasten off. Mark off 11 (12) mesh for each shoulder—17 mesh for neck edge.

RIGHT FRONT: Ch 73 (79). Work 4 rows border as for Back—71 (77) sts. *Row 5:* Ch 3, turn, dc in second sc and in each of next 5 sc—7 dc for front border; work in mesh pat across—21 (23) mesh. *Row 6:* Ch 5, turn, work across, dc in next 5 dc and top of ch-3 (border).

Note: When working from chart, *right,* read odd-numbered rows from right to left and even-numbered rows from left to right.

Row 7—Filet pat (right side): Ch 3, turn. Following Row 7 of chart, *right,* for right front, keeping 7 border sts, work 10 mesh, (2 dc in next ch-2 sp, 1 dc in next dc) twice—2 bls made, work across rem 9 (11) mesh.

Row 8: Ch 5, turn, work 8 (10) mesh, 4 bls, 9 mesh; end border sts.

Follow chart until motif is completed—26 rows (through Row 32). Work even, working only mesh sps and front border through Row 57.

Row 58: Following Chart, *right,* reading from left to right, dec 1 mesh pat as follows: **Work to within 2 mesh of border, ch 2, draw up lp in next dc, yo and draw through 2 lps, draw up lp in first dc of border, yo and draw through 2 lps, yo and draw through all 3 lps—dec made;** complete border—20 (22) mesh (including bls) rem.

Follow chart through Row 76, *and at same time,* dec 1 mesh pat as for Row 58 every second row until 11 (12) mesh rem. Work until same length as back to shoulder, end at front edge. Work on 7 border sts only until piece reaches around to center back neck edge; fasten off.

LEFT FRONT: Work as for Right Front; reverse shaping and charts.

SLEEVES: Ch 96. Work border as for Back for 4 rows. Work even in mesh pat for 47 rows, or desired length to underarm; fasten off.

FINISHING: Sew shoulder seams. Sew in sleeves between markers. Sew side seams. Sew center back border edges tog. Sew edges of back neckband to neck edge.

FILET JACKET

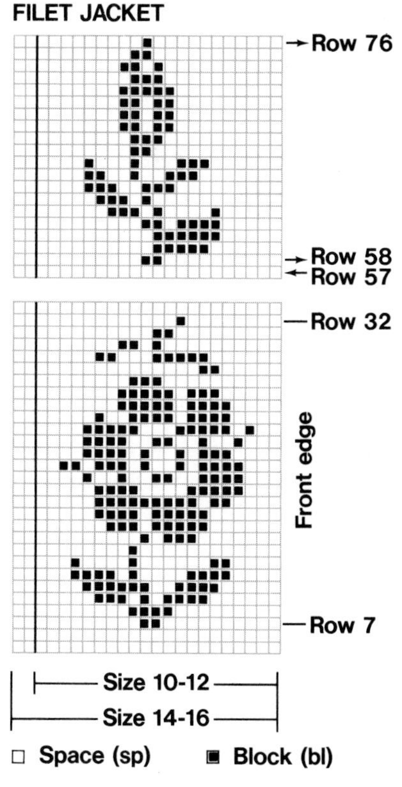

Child's Picture Pullover

Shown on pages 52–53.
Directions are for Size Small (4–6); changes for Size Medium (8–10) and Size Large (12–14) follow in parentheses. Chest = 25 (28, 33) inches.

MATERIALS
Unger Roly Poly (3½-ounce balls): 2 (2, 3) balls of No. 2749 blue; 1 (1, 1) ball *each* of No. 8352 green and No. 8001 white; small amounts of No. 2733 red, No. 1016 orange, No. 8011 yellow, No. 8767 black
Sizes 4 and 6 knitting needles or size to obtain gauge given below

Abbreviations: Page 217.
Gauge: With larger needles over st st, 5 sts = 1 inch; 7 rows = 1 inch.

INSTRUCTIONS: *Note on two-color knitting:* When changing colors in the middle of a row, always twist the new yarn around the one in use to prevent making holes in work. When carrying a strand of yarn across the back of work, twist it around the yarn in use every 3 sts.

BACK: With smaller needles and green, cast on 64 (70, 76) sts. Work in k 1, p 1 ribbing for 2 inches. Change to larger needles and st st (k 1 row, p 1 row). Work from Chart 1, *opposite,* for pat, adding blue as indicated on chart. Work even with blue until total length measures 11 (12, 13) inches, or desired length to underarm.

ARMHOLE SHAPING: Bind off 3 (4, 4) sts at beg of next 2 rows. Dec 1 st at beg of next 4 rows—54 (58, 64) sts. Work even until total length past beg of armhole measures 5½ (6, 6½) inches, ending with a p row.

SHOULDER SHAPING: Bind off 5 (6, 6) sts at beg of next 2 rows; then bind off 6 (6, 7) at beg of next 4 rows—20 (22, 24) sts. Sl rem sts to holder for back of neck.

FRONT: Work same as for Back, following Chart 2, *right,* for pat until total length past beg of armholes measures 3 (3½, 3¾) inches, ending with a p row—54 (58, 64) sts.

NECK SHAPING: Work across first 23 (24, 26) sts. Sl center 8 (10, 12) sts to holder for front of neck; join a second ball of yarn and complete row. Bind off 1 st each side of neck edge every other row 6 times. Work even until total length past beg of armholes measures same as for Back, ending with a p row. *For large size only,* continue in cloud pat at neck edge and with blue to complete neckline edge.

SHOULDER SHAPING: At each armhole edge, bind off 5 (6, 6) sts once, then bind off 6 (6, 7) sts twice.

SLEEVES: With smaller needles and green, cast on 36 (38, 40) sts. Work in k 1, p 1 ribbing for 2 inches. Change to larger needles and st st. Following Chart 3, *right,* inc 1 st each side every inch 6 (7, 8) times—48 (52, 56) sts, adding blue as required by pat. Work even using blue until total length measures 11 (12, 13) inches, or desired length to underarm.

TOP SHAPING: Bind off 3 (4, 4) sts at beg of every row until 10 (12, 12) sts rem. Bind off.

FINISHING: Sew left shoulder seam. With right side facing, smaller needles, and blue, k across 20 (22, 24) sts from back holder, pick up and k 21 (22, 22) sts along left neck edge, k 8 (10, 12) sts from front holder, pick up and k 21 (22, 22) sts along right neck edge—70 (76, 80) sts. Work in k 1, p 1 ribbing for 1 inch. Bind off loosely in ribbing. Sew right shoulder and neckband seam. Sew side and sleeve seams. Sew in sleeves, easing in fullness at top. Block.

Sailboat Sweaters

Shown on pages 54–55.
Directions are for Size Small (4–6); changes for Size Medium (8–10) follow in parentheses. Finished chest measurements = 26 (31) inches.

MATERIALS
For one sweater
Worsted-weight yarn (3½-ounce skeins): 2 (3) skeins of navy; 1 (1) skein *each* of red, green, and white
Several yards of gray
Sizes 6 and 8 knitting needles
Size 6 circular 16-inch needle
Knitting bobbins
Blunt-end tapestry needle

Abbreviations: Page 217.
Gauge: With larger needle over st st, 9 sts = 2 inches; 6 rows = 1 inch.

INSTRUCTIONS
BACK: With smaller straight needle and navy yarn, cast on 62 (70) sts. Work in k 1, p 1 ribbing for 2¼ inches. Change to larger needles and st st (k 1 row, p 1 row), and inc 6 sts evenly spaced across next row—68 (76) sts. Work even for 9 (10½) inches, or desired length to underarm.

ARMHOLE SHAPING: Bind off 2 sts at beg of next 4 rows. Bind off 1 st at beg of next 6 rows—54 (62) sts. Work even until length past beg of armholes measures 5¼ (6¼) inches, ending with a p row.

SHOULDER AND NECK SHAPING: Bind off 6 (7) sts at beg of next 2 rows. *Following row:* Knit 15 (17). Bind off center 12 (14) for neck, k 15 (17). Then bind off 5 (6) sts at shoulder edge. Bind off 4 sts at neck edge. Bind off rem 6 (7) sts. With wrong side facing, join yarn at opposite neck edge and p 15 (17). Bind off 5 (6) sts at beg of next row. Bind off 4 sts at beg of following row. Bind off rem 6 (7) sts.

FRONT: Work same as for Back until ribbing is completed. Change to larger needles and st st, inc 6 sts evenly on first row—68 (76) sts. For both sweaters work in st st for next 6 rows with navy.

For sweater with three sailboats

Fasten off navy; join red and begin to work 34 rows of pat from Chart 1, page 201. For ease in working, use bobbins for knitting the sailboat motifs, carrying blue across back of work. Gray masts and red sails may be knit in or added later using duplicate sts. Complete chart and continue to work even with navy until work is same length as Back to armholes. Begin armhole shapings and work as for Back until length past beg of armholes measures 3½ (4) inches, ending with a p row.

For sweater with one sailboat

Do not fasten off navy. Wind bobbins for each section of sailboat design to include navy bobbins for each side of sweater. Gray masts, red sails, sea gulls, and initial may be knit in or added later using duplicate sts. (See page 85 for duplicate stitch how-to.) Work 49 rows of boat design from Chart 2 and *at same time* when work is same length as Back to armholes, begin armhole shapings and work as for Back until length past beg of the armholes measures 3½ (4) inches, ending with a p row.

continued

For both sweaters

NECK SHAPING: K 22 (25), bind off center 10 (12) sts, k 22 (25). *Next row:* P across 22 sts. Continuing on the 22 sts, k, binding off 2 sts at neck edge, then dec 1 st at neck edge 3 times. Work even until length past beg of armholes measures 5¼ (6¼) inches.

SHOULDER SHAPING: Bind off 6 (7) sts at shoulder edge twice. Bind off rem 5 (6) sts.

Work other side of sweater neck shaping to correspond.

LONG SLEEVES: Cast on 30 (34) sts on smaller needle with navy yarn. Work in k 1, p 1 ribbing for 2 inches. Change to larger needles, (using red yarn for left sleeve and green yarn for right sleeve) and working in st st, inc 1 st at each end of first row and every other row 9 times—50 (54) sts. Work even until total length measures 12 (13) inches or desired length to underarm, ending with a p row. See below for Top Sleeve Shaping.

SHORT SLEEVES: Cast on 40 sts on smaller needles with navy yarn. Work in k 1, p 1 ribbing for 1 inch. Change to larger needles (using red yarn for left sleeve and green yarn for right sleeve) and inc 14 sts evenly spaced across row. Work even for 2½ inches or desired length for short sleeve underarm, ending with a p row. Work Top Sleeve Shaping, *below*, working numbers in ( )s for all sizes.

TOP SLEEVE SHAPING: Bind off 3 sts at beg of next 4 rows. Dec 1 st at beg and end of every other row 7 (9) times. Bind off 2 sts at beg of next 6 rows. Bind off rem 12 sts.

FINISHING: Following Chart 3, *opposite*, using duplicate sts and 1 strand of navy yarn, stitch the word "port" on red long sleeve and "starboard" on green long sleeve. Locate center 3 sts and begin stitching 16 rows down from top of sleeve for both words.

On large sailboat, loosely add a white strand of yarn from end of each sail to deck of boat.

Sew shoulder, side, and sleeve seams. Set in sleeves. With right sides facing and beg at shoulder seams, pick up and k 72 (84) sts with circular needles. Work in k 1, p 1 ribbing for 1 inch. Bind off loosely in ribbing.

Child's Sailboat Afghan

Shown on pages 56–57.
Finished size is 41x52 inches.

MATERIALS

Unger Roly Poly Yarn (3½-ounce balls): 8 balls of No. 1643 light blue; 4 balls *each* of No. 4556 medium blue and No. 6411 red; 3 balls of No. 1535/8468 burgundy; 1 ball *each* of No. 8011 yellow and No. 8001 white
Size H 22-inch-long afghan crochet hook
Size H aluminum crochet hook

Abbreviations: Page 211.
Gauge: 4 afghan sts = 1 inch.

INSTRUCTIONS

Note: Each complete row of afghan stitch consists of 2 parts—the first half of the row and the second half of the row.

With afghan hook and light blue, ch 155.

First half of Row 1: Retaining all lps on hook, sk first ch, * insert hook in next ch, yo, draw up lp; rep from * across row—155 lps on hook. *Second half of Row 1:* Yo and draw through first lp on hook, * yo, draw through next 2 lps on hook; rep from * until 1 lp rem on hook.

First half of Row 2: Insert hook under *second* vertical bar of Row 1, yo, draw up lp and leave on hook; * insert hook in next vertical bar, yo, draw up lp and leave on hook; rep from * across row to within 1 bar of end; insert hook under last bar and thread behind it, yo, draw up lp—155 lps on hook.

Second half of Row 2: Rep second half of Row 1.

Rows 3–12: Rep Row 2 (first and second halves); at end of Row 12 work until 2 lp rem on hook, drop light blue to back of work, with burgundy, yo, draw through last 2 lps on hook—color change made.

Continue to work as established, changing colors as cited above.

Rows 13–17: Work 5 rows with burgundy, changing to medium blue at end of Row 17.

Rows 18–41: Work 24 rows with medium blue, changing to red at end of Row 41. *Rows 42–46:* Work 5 rows with red, changing to light blue at end of Row 46.

Rows 47–54: Work 8 rows of light blue, changing to medium blue at end of Row 54. *Rows 55–56:* Work 2 rows with medium blue, changing to light blue at end of Row 56.

Rows 57–64: Work 8 rows with light blue, changing to burgundy at end of Row 64. *Rows 65–66:* Work 2 rows with burgundy, changing to light blue at end of Row 66.

Rows 67–74: Work 8 rows with light blue, changing to yellow at end of Row 74.

Rows 75–76: Work 2 rows with yellow, changing to light blue at end of Row 76.

Rows 77–84: Work 8 rows with light blue, changing to red at end of Row 84. *Rows 85–86:* Work 2 rows with red, changing to light blue at end of Row 86.

Work in reverse order (Rows 84–2) to complete opposite end.

Last row: Insert hook under *second* vertical bar, yo, draw up lp and pull through lp on hook—1 lp rem on hook; * insert hook in next vertical bar, yo, draw up lp and pull through lp on hook—1 lp on hook; rep from * across; fasten off.

continued

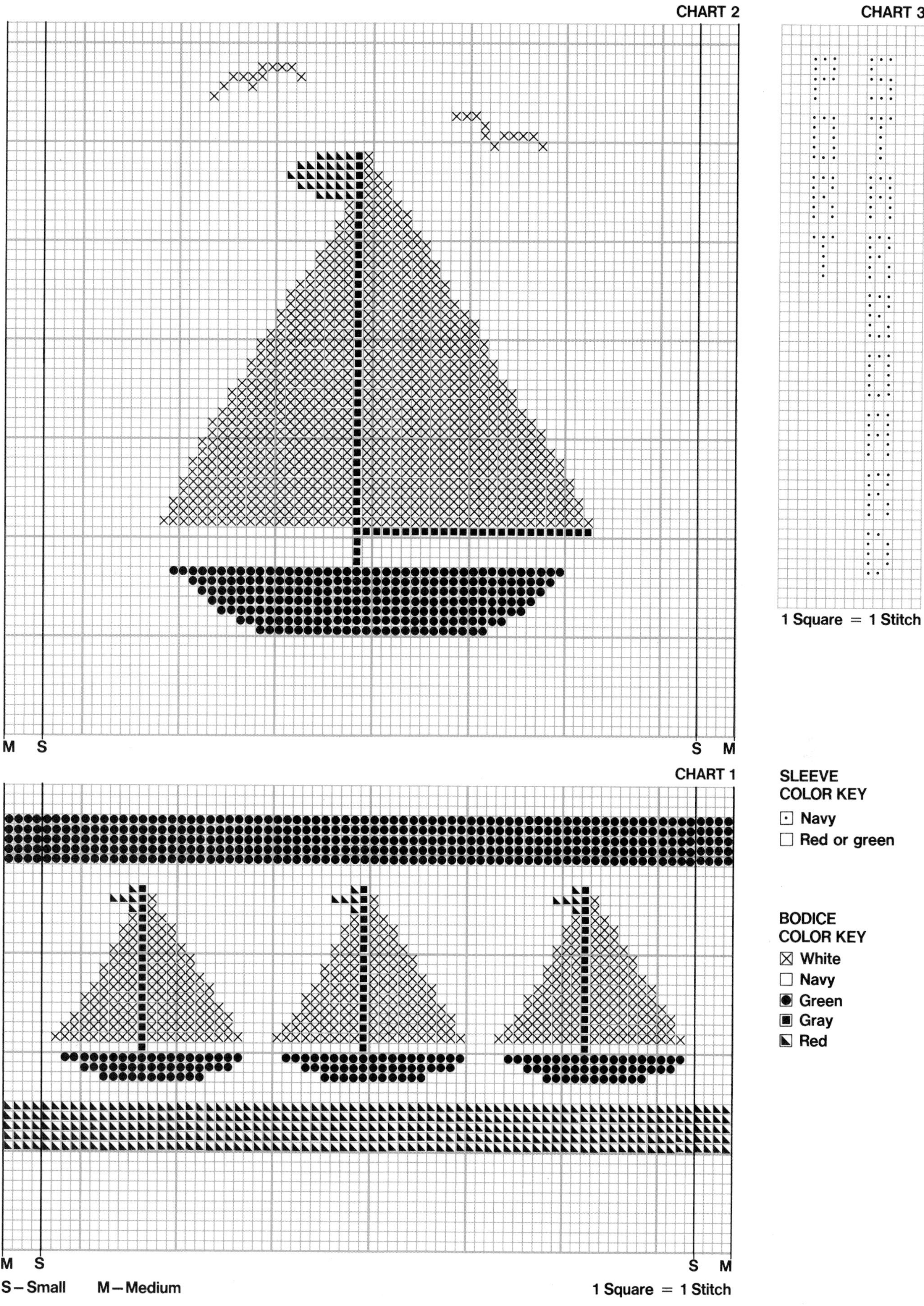

CHART 2
M
S
S
M
CHART 1
M
S
S
M
S–Small
M–Medium
1 Square = 1 Stitch
CHART 3
1 Square = 1 Stitch
SLEEVE
COLOR KEY
Navy
Red or green
BODICE
COLOR KEY
White
Navy
Green
Gray
Red

BORDER: *Rnd 1:* Join red in any st, ch 1, sc in same st as join. Work sc in each st around entire afghan, working 3 sc in each corner st; join with sl st to first sc.

Rnds 2–7: Ch 1, sc in same st as join, work as for Rnd 1; fasten off red at end of Rnd 7.

Rnd 8: Join burgundy in any sc, * ch 2; working *clockwise,* sk next 2 sc, sc in next sc; rep from * around; join to first sc. Fasten off.

CROSS-STITCH EMBROIDERY: Following Chart 1, page 201, work six sailboats in cross-stitches on both medium blue border strips at both ends of afghan. Use one strand of yarn to work over one vertical bar of afghan stitch. Refer to photograph, page 56, for working cross-stitches. To center the boats on the strip, allow 5 sts on each end and 5 sts *between* boats instead of 3 sts as shown on chart.

Knitted Amish Afghan

Shown on pages 106–107.
Finished size is 45x56 inches.

MATERIALS

Brunswick Windrush Yarn (3.5-ounce skeins): 7 skeins No. 90343, dark brown; 2 skeins *each* No. 90423 cranberry and No. 90593 dark jade
Size 8 circular knitting needle (36-inch length)
Size G crochet hook
Size 8 straight knitting needles
Point protectors

Abbreviations: Pages 211 and 217.
Gauge: 5 sts = 1 inch; 7 rows = 1 inch

INSTRUCTIONS

PATTERN A: Basket-Weave St (multiple of 8 sts over 232 sts). *Row 1* (wrong side): K 3, * p 2, k 6; rep from *; end p 2, k 3.

Row 2: P 3, * k 2, p 6; rep from *; end k 2, p 3.

Row 3: Rep Row 1. *Row 4:* Knit all sts. *Row 5:* K 7, * p 2, k 6, rep from *; end p 2, k 7.

Row 6: P 7, * k 2, p 6, rep from *; end k 2, p 7.

Row 7: Rep Row 5. *Row 8:* Knit all sts. Rep Rows 1–8 for pat.

PATTERN A: Basket-Weave St (multiple of 8 sts over 30 sts)

Row 1: K 3, (p 2, k 6) 3 times; end p 2, k 1.

Row 2: P 1, (k 2, p 6) 3 times, end k 2, p 3.

Row 3: Rep Row 1. *Row 4:* K all sts. *Row 5:* K 7, (p 2, k 6) twice; end p 2, k 5.

Row 6: P 5, (k 2, p 6) twice; end k 2, p 7.

Row 7: Rep Row 5. *Row 8:* Knit all sts. Rep Rows 1–8 for pat.

PATTERN B: Seed St (over odd number of sts)

Row 1: * K 1, p 1; rep from * ending k 1. Rep Row 1 for pat.

PAT C: Triangular Stitch (multiple of 7 sts)

Row 1: * P 6, k 1; rep from *.
Row 2: * P 2, k 5; rep from *.
Row 3: * P 4, k 3; rep from *.
Row 4: * P 4, k 3; rep from *.
Row 5: * P 2, k 5; rep from *.
Row 6: * P 6, k 1; rep from *.
Rep Rows 1–6 for pat.

PATTERN D: Hurdle St (multiple of 2 sts)

Row 1: Knit. *Row 2:* Knit.
Rows 3–4: * K 1, p 1; rep from *.
Rep Rows 1–4 for pat.

With circular needle and brown, cast on 232 sts. Work Rows 1–8 of Pat A; then rep Rows 1–8 of Pat A 5 times more, ending with Row 7 on last rep.

Next row: Knit across 30 sts, drop brown, join cranberry, k 1, inc in next st, k to last 30 sts, drop cranberry, attach a second ball of brown and k rem 30 sts.

Work Row 1 of Pat A with brown over 30 sts; then work Pat B over 173 sts with cranberry, complete row with brown in Pat A over rem 30 sts.

Continue working Pat A (over 30 sts), and Pat B until 8 rows of Pat A are worked 9 times from the cast-on edge, ending last repeat with Row 7.

Next row: With straight needles work across 30 sts in Row 8 of Pat A. Put point protectors on both ends of circular needle. Working with straight needles continue working on 30 sts until there are 46 repeats of Pat A from cast on, ending with Row 7. Sl sts to holder.

Break off brown.

Working in Pat B, with cranberry and straight needle, work across next 15 sts on circular needle; replace point protector on circular needle.

With straight needles and cranberry over 15 sts, work Pat B until same length as first strip. Sl 15 sts to holder. Break off cranberry.

With straight needle and dark jade, k across next 21 sts on circular needle. Work Pat C on 21 sts with jade until 49 repeats of Pat C completed. Sl sts to holder. Break off jade.

With straight needle and brown, k across next 19 sts on circular needle and at same time, inc 1 st in middle of row—20 sts on needle. Work in Pat D on 20 sts with brown until 73 repeats of Pat D completed. Sl sts to holder. Break off brown.

With straight needle and dark jade, k across next 21 sts on circular needle. Work in Pat C on 21 sts with jade until 49 repeats of Pat C completed. Sl sts to holder. Break off jade.

With straight needle and brown, k across next 20 sts on circular needle. Work in Pat D on 20 sts with brown until 73 repeats of Pat D completed. Sl sts to holder. Break off brown.

With straight needle and dark jade, k across next 21 sts on circular needle. Work in Pat C on 21 sts with jade until 49 repeats of Pat C are completed. Sl sts to holder. Break off jade.

Repeat last 2 strips—there are 4 jade Pat C strips and 3 brown Pat D strips.

K across next 15 sts on circular needle in cranberry and work in Pat B until strip measures same length as rem strips. Sl sts to holder. Break off cranberry.

Work Pat A with brown on rem 30 sts until 46 pat repeats are completed, ending with Row 7. Taking care to untwist all strips, transfer all sts back on to circular needle. With right side facing, work as follows: K across 30 sts with brown. K across next 9 strips (174 sts) with cranberry and *at same time,* dec 1 st with cranberry—173 cranberry sts. Attach a second ball of brown and knit across last 30 sts.

Next row: With brown, work across 30 sts in Row 1 of Pat A; with cranberry, work across 173 sts in Pat B; with brown, work across rem 30 sts in Row 1 of Pat A. Continue in this manner until there are 49 repeats of Pat A from cast-on edge, ending with Row 7. Break off cranberry and second ball of brown.

Continue with brown and Row 8 of Pat A, work across all sts and dec 1 st in middle of row—232 sts on needle. Continue with brown and Pat A for 6 more complete patterns. Bind off loosely. Whipstitch all center strips together and steam lightly. Tie in all ends.

EDGING: *Rnd 1:* With right side facing, join brown yarn at lower left corner of cast-on edge and sc around entire afghan as follows: Work 3 sc in corner st, sc in each cast on st to next corner, 3 sc in corner st, 4 sc in *each* pat rep along long edge, 3 sc in next corner; work rem 2 sides to correspond; join to first sc. Fasten off.

Rnd 2: Join cranberry in any sc, ch 3, work dc in each sc around; in center st of 3-sc corner grp work 2 dc, ch 1, 2 dc; join to top of ch-3.

Rnd 3: Ch 3, dc in each dc around; in ch-1 corner sp work 2 dc, ch 1, 2 dc; join to top of ch-3.

Rnd 4: Ch 2, * **trc from front around post of next dc 2 rows below—raised trc made,** sk dc behind raised trc, hdc in next dc, rep from * to corner; in ch-1 corner sp work 2 hdc, ch 1, 2 hdc; rep from first * around; join to top of ch-2 at beg of rnd.

Rnd 5: Ch 1, sc in same st as join; * sc in each dc to corner; in ch-1 corner sp work 2 sc, ch 1, 2 sc; rep from * around; join to first sc.

Rnd 6: Ch 1, working clockwise (reverse single crochet), sc in each sc around and 3 sc in each ch-1 corner sp; join to first sc; fasten off.

Crocheted Amish Afghan

Shown on pages 104–105.
Finished size is 42 inches square.

MATERIALS

Brunswick Knitting Worsted (3.5-ounce skeins): 3 skeins No. 4131 bright navy; 2 skeins *each* No. 422 garnet and No. 4362 ocher; 1 skein *each* No. 424 cardinal, No. 491 blackberry heather, and No. 4125 dark copenhagen blue

Size G aluminum crochet hook

Abbreviations: See page 211.
Gauge: 7 sc = 2 inches.

INSTRUCTIONS

CENTER SQUARE: Beg at center, with scarlet, ch 5; join with sl st to form ring.

Rnd 1: Work 12 sc in ring; mark last sc for end of rnd (do not join).

Rnd 2: Working in back loops until specified otherwise, sc in next sc; * 3 sc in next sc—corner made; sc in each of next 2 sc; rep from * 2 times more; end 3 sc in next sc, sc in last sc—20 sc made.

Rnd 3: Moving marker at the end of each rnd, sc in each of next 2 sc; * 3 sc in next sc, sc in each of next 4 sc; rep from * two times more; ending 3 sc in next sc, sc in last 2 sc—28 sc made.

Rnd 4: Sc in each of next 3 sc; * 3 sc in next sc, sc in each of next 6 sc; rep from * 2 times more; ending 3 sc in next sc, sc in next 3 sc—36 sc.

Rnd 5: Sc in each of next 4 sc; * 3 sc in next sc, sc in each of next 8 sc; rep from * 2 times more; ending 3 sc in next sc, sc in each of next 4 sc—44 sc made.

Continue around piece in this manner until 40 sc from corner to corner are made. Work should measure approximately 11 inches square.

BORDER: *Row 1:* Working under both lps, with wrong side facing, join blackberry heather in center sc of any corner, ch 3, dc in each sc across row; ending dc in center sc of next corner—40 dc, counting beg ch-3 as dc; ch 3, turn.

Row 2: Sk first dc, dc around post of next dc *from front;* * dc around post of each of next 2 dc *from back,* dc around post of each of next 2 dc *from front;* rep from * across row working last dc in top of turning ch; ch 2, turn.

Row 3: Sk first dc, dc around post of next dc *from back;* * dc around post of each of next 2 dc *from front,* dc around post of each of next 2 dc *from back;* rep from * across row working last dc in top of turning ch; ch 2, turn.

Rows 4–7: Repeat rows 2–3 two times more.

Row 8: Rep Row 2. Fasten off. Rep Border instructions on rem 3 sides.

CORNER BLOCKS: *Row 1:* With copenhagen blue and right side facing, join copenhagen blue around turning ch (dc) at outside edge of any blackberry strip, ch 1, sc in same st as join; * ch 1, sk ¼ inch on blackberry strip, sc around turning ch-lp; rep from * 6 times more—8 sc in row; ch 1, turn.

Row 2: Sc in first sc, sc in next ch-1 sp; * ch 1, sk next sc, sc in next ch-1 sp; rep from * to last sc; sc in last sc; ch 1, turn.

continued

Row 3: Sc in first sc; * ch 1, sk sc, sc in next ch-1 sp; rep from * to last 2 sc; ch 1, sk sc, sc in last sc; ch 1, turn.

Rep Rows 2–3 until length equals length of blackberry strip, ending at inside edge; fasten off, leaving 12-inch strand of yarn and whipstitch to adjoining blackberry strip.

Rep Corner Block for rem 3 corners.

TRIANGULAR SECTIONS: With right side facing, join garnet in end st of any blue corner block. *Row 1:* Ch 3, sk 2 sts, **3 dc in next st—shell made;** work 21 more shells evenly spaced across row, ending with dc in last st at end of blue block—22 shells made; ch 3, turn.

Row 2: (Shell in sp bet next 2 shells) 21 times; dc in sp bet last shell and turning-ch; ch 3, turn.

Rows 3–22: Rep Row 2—there will be one less shell on each row and 1 shell at end of Row 22; do not ch 3 at end of Row 22; fasten off.

Rep triangular sections on rem 3 sides. Block work at this point if necessary. Lay finished piece on a flat surface and cover with wet towel; allow to dry completely.

OCHER BORDER: *Rnd 1:* With right side facing, join ocher in center st of any corner; ch 1, 3 sc in same corner st; * in each turning-ch-lp work 2 sc to next corner, sk first dc in corner 3-dc grp, 3 sc in next dc; rep from * 3 times more, ending with sl st in first sc at beg of rnd.

Rnd 2: Sl st in next sc, ch 1, 3 sc in same sc as sl st; * sk sc, sc in next sc, sc in sc just skipped, sk st already worked in; rep from * across row to center sc of corner grp; 3 sc in center sc; rep from first * across row and work rem 3 sides to correspond; end with sl st in first sc at beg of rnd.

Rep Rnd 2 until border measures 2½ inches.

NAVY BORDER: *Rnd 1:* With right side facing, join navy in center sc on any 3 sc-grp, ch 1, sc in same st; ch 3, in same st work 3 dc; * in next st work **sc, ch 3, 3 dc—slanted shell made;** sk next 3 sts; rep from * across to 3-sc corner grp. **(In next sc work sc, ch 3, 3 dc) 3 times—corner made;** sk next 3 sts; rep from first * across next side to 3 corner sts; work corner. Work rem 2 sides to correspond; ending sc in last sc in rnd, ch 3, 3 dc in same st to complete first corner; join with sl st to first sc at beg of rnd; ch 3, turn.

Rnd 2: * Sk next 3 dc, in next ch-3 lp work sc, ch 3, 3 dc; rep from * around; join with sl st to first sc at beg of rnd (following the ch-3 lp); ch 1, turn.

Place markers on ch-3 lps of other 3 corners to establish corners.

Rnd 3: In same st as join work sc, ch 3, 3-dc (place marker on sc just made); * in next ch-3 lp work sc, ch 3, 3 dc; rep from * to marked corner lp; in corner lp work sc, ch 3, 3 dc (place marker on sc); in sc following the marked shell make sc, ch 3, 3 dc; rep from first * to next marked corner lp; work sc, ch 3, 3 dc in marked lp (place marker on sc); work rem 2 sides to correspond; join with sl st to first sc; ch 3, turn.

Rnd 4: Rep Rnd 2; ch 3, turn.

Rnd 5: Work slanted shell in next ch-3 lp, work slanted shell in next sc (mark sc for corner); * work slanted shell in each ch-3 lp to marked sc; slanted shell in next sc (mark sc for corner); rep from * around; join with sl st to first sc; ch 3, turn.

Rnds 6–9: Rep Rnds 2–3 alternately; end of Rnd 9 sl st in top of ch-3, ch 1, turn.

Rnd 10: * Sc in next 3 dc and into ch-3 lp, ch 2; rep from * around, ending sl st in first sc; fasten off.

CARDINAL BORDER: *Rnd 1:* With right side facing, join cardinal in any sc; ch 3, dc in each dc around (sk the ch-2 lps). In corners work 2 dc in ch-2 lps as necessary. *Note:* Corners are not square; work dcs in lps only to make work lie flat. Join to top of ch-3 at beg of rnd.

Rnd 2: Ch 1, sc in same st as join, work sc in each dc around; join to first sc; fasten off. Block again.

Filet Crochet Curtain Valance

Shown on pages 108–109.
Finished size is 20x50 inches.

MATERIALS

Clark's Big Ball Crochet Cotton, Size 30 (350-yard balls): 5 balls of white or ecru
Size 12 steel crochet hook
1-inch-wide grosgrain ribbon or bias tape for heading

Abbreviations: Page 211.
Gauge: 5 spaces and 6 rows = 1 inch.

INSTRUCTIONS

Curtain is worked lengthwise. Any length may be worked by repeating floral pattern until necessary width is obtained. To begin, ch about 315 sts.

Row 1: Dc in eighth ch from hook, * ch 2, sk 2 ch, dc in next ch; rep from * until 98 sps made. Dc in each of next 3 ch—block made; ch 2, sk 2 ch, dc in next ch. Cut off rem ch about an inch from end of work and ravel back to last dc made and weave in end. Ch 10, turn.

Row 2: Dc in eighth ch from hook, ch 2, dc in next dc, 2 dc in next ch-2 sp, dc in next dc, ch 2, sk 2 dc; * dc in next dc, ch 2; rep from * across; end sk 2 ch of turning ch, dc in next ch; ch 5, turn.

Row 3: (Dc in next dc, ch 2) 99 times, ch 2, sk 2 dc, dc in next dc, 2 dc in next ch-2 sp, dc in next dc, ch 2, sk 2 ch of turning ch, dc in next ch; ch 10, turn.

continued

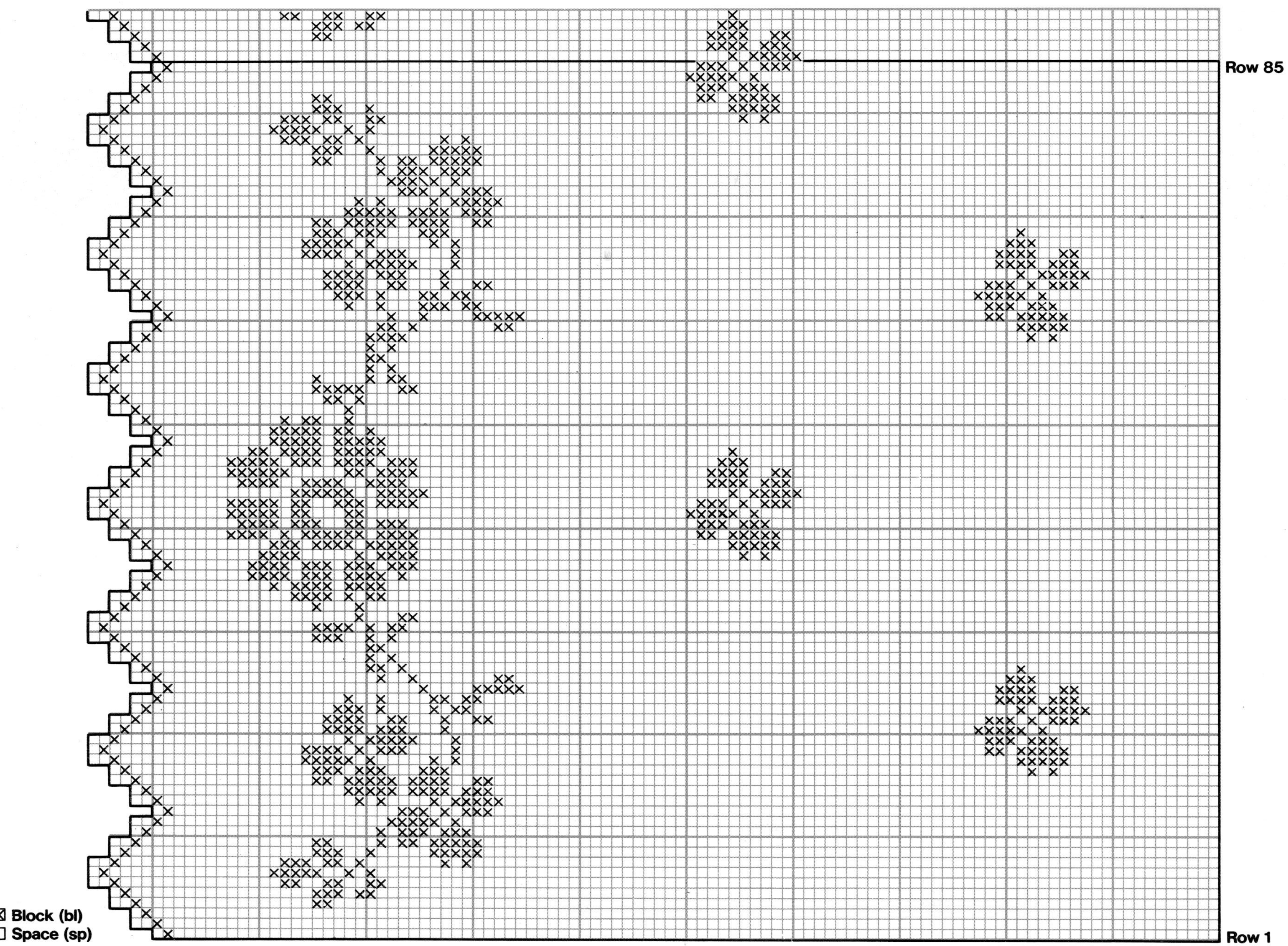
Row 85
Row 1
☒ Block (bl)
☐ Space (sp)

Row 4: Dc in eighth ch from hook, ch 2, dc in next dc, 2 dc in ch-2 sp, dc in next dc, ch 2, sk 2 dc, dc in next dc; work from chart, page 205, to complete row; ch 5, turn.

Note: Refer to page 205 to work all references to chart in instructions that follow.

Row 5: Work from chart, ending row as for Row 3; ch 10, turn.

Row 6: Dc in eighth ch from hook, ch 2, dc in next dc, 2 dc in next ch-2 sp, dc in next dc; work from chart to complete row; ch 5, turn.

Row 7: Work from chart; end ch 5, turn.

Row 8: Dc in next dc, ch 2, sk 2 dc, dc in next dc, 2 dc in ch-2 sp, dc in next dc; work from chart to complete row.

Continue to work from chart through Row 85; complete motif already established *and at the same time,* rep Rows 2–85 twice more or for desired width, omitting last small floral motif on last rep; do not fasten off.

FINISHING: Work scs around ch-lps and dcs on all sides of curtain valance, taking care to keep work flat; join to first sc; fasten off. Wash, starch, and steam-press valance. Machine-stitch ribbon or bias tape along top edge for rod pocket.

Crocheted Oval Place Mat and Rug

Shown on pages 154–155.
Finished place mat measures 11x18 inches. Finished rug is 40½x24½ inches.

MATERIALS
For the place mat
Lily Double Quick 100% Cotton (115-yard balls): 1 ball No. 29 delft blue; 2 balls of No. 1 white
Size 1 steel crochet hook

For the rug
White and blue fabric cut into ¾-inch strips
Size K aluminum crochet hook

Abbreviations: Page 211.

INSTRUCTIONS
For the place mat

Starting in center, with white, ch 39.

Rnd 1: Work 2 sc in second ch from hook and sc in each ch across; 3 sc in last ch. Working along opposite side of starting ch, work sc in each ch across, sc in same st with first 2 sc. Join with sl st to first sc.

Rnd 2: Ch 3, dc in same st as sl st, 3 dc in next 2 sc, dc in next 34 sc, 3 dc in each of next 5 sc, dc in next 34 sc, 3 dc in next 2 sc, dc in same st as first dc. Join with st st to top of ch-3 at beg of rnd. Draw blue through lp on hook, drop white to back of work.

Rnd 3: With blue, sc in same st as sl st; * ch 3, sl st in last sc for picot, sc in next 2 dc; rep from * around. Join to first sc. Draw white through lp on hook, drop blue to back.

Rnd 4: Working behind picots, (sc in back lp of first sc between next 2 picots, 2 sc in next sc—inc made) 4 times; * sc in back lps of 2 sc between next 2 picots; rep from * across, make 8 incs around end, work even across next side, work 4 incs around final curve, join to first sc.

Rnd 5: Ch 3, working in both lps, (make 2 dc in next sc—inc made, dc in next sc) 4 times, dc in each sc around with 9 incs around other end and 5 more incs around final curve. Join to top of ch-3.

Rnd 6: Ch 3, dc in each dc around, inc 9 dc on both ends of rnd. Join, pull blue through lp on hook.

Rnd 7: Rep Rnd 3.

Rnd 8: Rep Rnd 4, making sc in each sc around (without inc).

Rnd 9: Rep Rnd 5 with 10 incs around each end.

Rnd 10: Rep Rnd 6 with 11 incs around each end.

Rnd 11: Rep Rnd 3.

Rnd 12: Rep Rnd 4 with 11 incs around each end.

Rnd 13: Rep Rnd 5 with 11 incs around each end.

Rnd 14: Rep Rnd 6 with 7 incs around each end.

Rnd 15: Rep Rnd 3.

Rnd 16: Rep Rnd 8.

Rnds 17–18: Rep Rnds 5–6 with 6 incs around each end.

Rnds 19–20: Rep Rnds 3 and 8.

Rnd 21: Rep Rnd 5 with 7 incs around each end.

Rnd 22: Rep Rnd 6 with 9 incs around each end. Fasten off white.

Rnd 23: Rep Rnd 3. Fasten off blue; block.

For the rug

Working inc in curves only as many times as necessary to keep work lying flat, work rug according to instructions for oval place mat, *above.*

Straw Hat With Flowers

Shown on page 155.

MATERIALS
Purchased straw hat
DMC Pearl Cotton, Size 8 (95-yard balls): 1 ball *each* of No. 747 light blue, No. 809 dark blue, No. 554 light lavender, No. 553 dark lavender, No. 727 yellow, No. 353 light peach, No. 352 dark peach
Size 8 steel crochet hook
2 yards of 1½-inch-wide blue satin ribbon
3 packages of purchased velvet leaves
3 packages of purchased pearl calyxes
Floral tape and wire

Abbreviations: Page 211.

INSTRUCTIONS

The rose and pansy flowers for hat are made from instructions on page 120. For hat, we made a total of 15 roses and six pansies. Using the rose pat and the two shades of peach, make 3 sizes. For the largest rose, work 9 rnds; the medium rose, work 7 rnds; the small rose, work 5 rnds. For the yellow centers, work 3 rnds. Work the pansy with two shades of blue and lavender.

Place a pearl calyx through center of flowers and wrap the stem with floral tape. Fasten velvet leaves to stems with floral tape.

The small filler flowers (make 25) are worked with blue and lavender threads as follows: Ch 4, trc in fourth ch from hook, ch 3, sl st in third ch from hook, ch 4, sl st in same ch used for trc—petal made. (Ch 4, trc in same ch used for first trc, ch 3, sl st in third ch from hook, ch 4, sl st in same ch) 4 times; fasten off.

Separate the pearl calyxes and use one small pearl as flower center. Use wire for stems and wrap with floral tape.

Cut a long piece of wire to fit ¾ of way around base of hat and fasten flowers and remaining pearl calyxes to wire with tape in a pleasing arrangement. Staple wire to hat.

From ribbon, make bow with streamers and fasten to hat in area uncovered with wire. Tuck in flowers and pearls around bow.

Jacket with Knitted Sleeves

Shown on pages 156–157.

MATERIALS

Purchased pattern for jacket or vest
Fabrics and notions as listed on pattern
Worsted-weight yarn (3½-ounce skeins): For a tweed effect, 2 skeins *each* of 2 yarn colors to coordinate with fabric. For solid-color sleeves, 3 skeins of yarn to match fabric
Size 10 knitting needles

Abbreviations: Page 217.
Gauge: 4 sts = 1 inch with 2 strands of yarn.

INSTRUCTIONS

For ease in determining sleeve opening and to ensure knitted sleeves will fit sewn garment, trace onto stiff paper upper quarter of jacket front and back from shoulder to 2 inches below sleeve. Cut patterns from paper and tape shoulder and underarm seams. When sleeves are completed, fit sleeve into paper pattern and make any adjustments to paper pattern as necessary before cutting fabric. In our jacket, we cut away ⅜-inch of fabric around the shoulder and underarms for fitting in sleeves. This knitted sleeve has a lot of give, so allow for easing when sewing sleeve to fabric.

Using sleeve pattern for woman's cardigan, page 71, work size to correspond with jacket pattern. Use two strands of yarn held together as directed in sleeve instructions.

Assemble jacket or vest according to pattern instructions. Do not finish sleeve edges or attach lining to sleeve until knitted sleeves are sewn into jacket. Pin, baste, then machine-sew sleeves to jacket fabric leaving lining free. Turn under the seam allowance of the sleeve lining and hand-sew over raw seams to complete.

Knitted Fair Isle And Aran Afghan

Shown on pages 158–159.
Finished size is 42x57 inches.

MATERIALS

Unger Aires Worsted Yarn (3½-ounce balls): 9 balls of No. 469 gray; 1 ball *each* of No. 454 camel (A), No. 426 green (B), No. 403 grape (C), No. 437 yellow (D), No. 417 blue (E)
Sizes 8 and 9 knitting needles
Cable needle

Abbreviations: Page 217.
Gauge: With larger needles over st st, 4 sts = 1 inch.

INSTRUCTIONS

CENTER PANEL: The center panel is worked using the Back instructions, pages 82 and 83, for the Fair Isle vest shown on page 66. With Size 8 needles, cast on 100 sts; work double row of seed st for 12 rows for border. Change to larger needles and pat st and work as for Back as follows: When working Pat 1, work first 3 sts in gray, then begin to work Pat 1 across row, ending with 3 sts in gray.

When working rem Pat (rows 2–6), work first 2 sts in gray, then begin to work pat, ending with 2 sts in gray.

Rep Pats 1–6 three times, changing colors each time you rep the pat as shown on diagram, page 82; then rep Pat 1 with the first color rep. Change to Size 8 needles and work 12 rows of double seed st; bind off.

SIDE PANEL (make 2): Use the Sleeve instructions, page 46, for the Irish knit pullover sweater shown on pages 38 and 39. With Size 8 needles, cast on 44 sts; work double row of seed st for 12 rows. Change to larger needles and Aran Pat, establish pat as follows: *Row 1:* Double moss st over 8 sts, p 1, cable over 6 sts, p 1, zigzag over 1 st, p 1, spoon st over 8 sts, p 1, zigzag over 1 st, p 1, cable over 6 sts, p 1, double moss over 8 sts. Continuing with Row 2 of all pats, work in pat until length is same as center panel less the border. Change to smaller needles and work 12 rows of double seed st; bind off.

FINISHING: With gray, whipstitch panels together. Fold and knot five 10-inch multicolored strands of yarn into every other st across the short sides of the afghan. Block to complete.

STITCHER'S NOTEBOOK

Here, and on the next 11 pages, you will find information and tips to assist you in developing your knitting and crocheting techniques and to enhance your enjoyment of these two needlecrafts.

Hooks and needles

Hooks and needles are available in many different materials—wood, plastic, aluminum, and for crochet, steel. They are all sized to work with different thicknesses of yarn or thread. Keep several sizes of hooks and needles available to adjust your gauge easily to conform to pattern instructions.

CROCHET HOOKS: The smallest hooks, used primarily with fine, lace-weight thread, are steel and about five inches long. The sizes are numbered from 00, 0, and 1 through 14. The larger the number (Size 14, for example), the smaller the hook; the lower the number, the larger the hook.

Aluminum and plastic hooks are larger than steel hooks and are sized by letters from C (the smallest), through K (the largest). They are about six inches long and are used for working with yarns.

Wooden hooks—used with thick yarns—are available in sizes 10, 14, and 15. They are nine inches long.

Afghan hooks, which resemble knitting needles except that they have a hook instead of a point on one end, are used to work the afghan stitch. They are made of aluminum and are sized the same as regular aluminum and plastic hooks. Afghan hooks are available in 9-, 14-, and 22-inch lengths. For afghan stitch projects, select a hook that is long enough to hold all the stitches in the individual rows.

KNITTING NEEDLES: Like crochet hooks, knitting needles come in many sizes and lengths. They are made from the same materials—wood, plastic, and aluminum. The three most common types are the *standard* needle with a stopper at one end and a point at the other end, the *double-pointed* needle, which is pointed on both ends, and the *circular* needle, which has points at each end and a flexible cord between. Sizes for all three types range from Size 2, the smallest, through Size 13, the largest.

Use standard needles for flat knitting (knitting in rows), but use double-pointed and circular needles for seamless knitting (knitting in rounds). You may also use circular needles for flat knitting; they are particularly practical for patterns with many stitches in the rows.

Choosing yarns

Yarns and threads are made from natural fibers, synthetics, and blends. When spun into different thicknesses or subjected to special treatments, yarns acquire their own characteristics of weight (or thickness) and texture.

Yarns fall into approximately four groups, according to weight: sock or baby yarns, sport yarns, worsted yarns, and bulky yarns. Each of these weights can be sorted into grades of quality depending upon the fibers from which they are spun or the dyes used to color them. Some will be more resistant than others to pilling, felting, or fading.

Before purchasing yarn, determine the project you plan to stitch so you buy yarn with the fiber content, care requirements, weight, and texture appropriate for that project.

Always purchase enough yarn (or slightly more) to make the article. Yarns are dyed in huge lots at one time and no two dye lots are ever the same. To avoid disappointment, always check the labels when you buy yarn to ensure that all of it is from the same dye lot.

Substituting yarn

Any yarn can be substituted for any other yarn, provided you can work it to the gauge specified in the pattern. If you want your project to look like the project pictured, select a yarn similar in weight and texture to the yarn in the materials list.

When substituting, determine how much of the new yarn you will need. First, multiply the number of yards per skein in the *pattern* yarn by the number of skeins required. Then, divide this number by the number of yards per skein of the *substitute* yarn to determine the number of skeins needed in the new yarn.

Working the gauge

Most knitting and crocheting patterns include a *gauge* notation. Gauge, or the number of stitches or rows per inch, is normally determined by the *hook* or *needle size*, not by the weight of the yarn.

Always work a gauge swatch to see if your tension using the specified yarn and hook or needle equals the gauge cited. Using the dominant pattern stitch in the project, crochet or knit a swatch at least four inches square. Then in the center of the swatch, count the number of stitches for two inches, and divide by two to get your gauge for one inch.

If you have too many stitches per inch (more than the gauge specified in the instructions), you are working too tightly. You need to stitch with less tension or change to a *larger* hook or needle.

If you have too few stitches per inch, you are working too loosely. You need to stitch with tighter tension or change to a *smaller* hook or needle. Keep changing your hook or needle until your gauge is correct.

Reading instructions

Following instructions may seem difficult as you begin. Pay attention to commas, semicolons, and periods. Knitting and crocheting are worked in steps and each step is set off by punctuation.

Also, knitting and crocheting instructions are written in an abbreviated form. Familiarize yourself with these abbreviations before beginning a project (see pages 211 and 217).

Symbols are used to shorten directions and to indicate that a section of a pattern is repeated. Asterisks (*) indicate pattern repeats within a row or round. Asterisks are used in groups of two; when there is a beginning one, there also will be an ending one. Work the stitches *between* the asterisks, then *repeat* the pattern between the asterisks as many times as indicated. For example, if the pattern indicates you are to repeat between the asterisks two times more, you will actually work the stitches between the asterisks a total of three times.

Double asterisks (**) are sometimes used to set off a string of instructions that also requires single asterisks within the same set of pattern repetition. Read these instructions the same as for the single set of asterisks.

Parentheses ( ), and brackets [ ] also indicate repetition. Repeat the instructions within the parentheses or brackets the total number of times indicated before beginning the next step in the instructions. Work the stitches within parentheses or brackets *only as many times as specified.*

Working with bobbins

Changing colors is simple when you stitch with bobbins because you need not carry an entire ball of yarn for every color in the design.

Bobbins generally are available in two sizes. Use the smaller size for baby, fingering, sock, and other lightweight yarns and the larger for sport, worsted, or bulky yarns.

To determine how much yarn to wind on a bobbin, estimate the width of the area you plan to stitch in a color; wind four times as much yarn onto the bobbin.

Use a separate bobbin for each color, except the main color, in the design you are stitching.

To fill the bobbin, wrap the yarn *horizontally* around the bobbin three times, and then wrap it *vertically* once to fasten it into the slot. Continue winding in this way until you've wound all the yarn or filled the bobbin. Avoid overloading the bobbin. It is better to tie in another bobbin at a convenient point in your work than to wrap yarn too tightly or too full. Join the new bobbin at a point where colors change or at a place where joining will not be obvious.

When *knitting,* as you work across the row and come to the next color, drop the color in use on the side the stitch ends (knits at back of work, purls at front of work). With the right hand, pick up the new color from *beneath* the old one and work the next stitch. Bringing the new yarn *under* the old yarn twists the yarns together and makes a loop that prevents a hole where the two colors join.

Maintain your regular working tension when changing colors between the stitches; do not pull these stitches tightly.

When *crocheting,* work up to the stitch before the color change, then work the next stitch to the point where there are two loops on the hook. Drop the color in use and with the next color, wrap the yarn over the hook (yo) and draw the yarn through the remaining two loops on the hook. Always drop the last bobbin used to the front side as the work faces you.

A word of caution: As convenient as they are, bobbins can only be used when you are knitting or crocheting in *rows.* You cannot work in *rounds* with bobbins because at the end of a round the bobbin will be at the *end* of the color area (rather than the beginning) when you start the next round of stitches.

Finishing techniques

SEAMING: Sew seams with the yarn used in the project, except when the project yarn is nubby, thick and thin, or bulky. For projects made with these yarns, select a smooth, medium-weight yarn in a matching color. If the color is difficult to match, use crewel yarns; they are available in a range of colors and can be separated into strands.

The tension of all seam finishes must be tight enough to hide the joining stitches, but loose enough to be as elastic as the finished item.

To join, pin two sections together, matching designs or patterns. Join, using backstitches, overcast stitches, or whipstitches.

Backstitches are firm and strong, but they must be worked at the correct tension because they have little "give" once in place. Whipstitches or overcast stitches result in a flat, almost invisible seam; they are especially useful for joining motifs such as Granny Squares. Whipstitches work best on knitted panels with seed- or garter-stitch edges.

FINISHING ENDS: When breaking off yarn ends, leave at least a 6-inch tail for weaving. When working in rows, weave yarn ends into the seam allowances whenever possible. When working in rounds, weave ends *vertically* to make them less noticeable on the right side.

Split the ends of bulky yarns and weave each ply separately for a finer appearance on the right side.

BLOCKING: Before blocking, check the label of the yarn you are using; you may find the yarn requires no blocking. If blocking is needed, follow the manufacturer's instructions.

Projects may be blocked before or after seaming. To block before seaming, pin matching pieces to identical shape and size. Depending on the fiber content, place a wet or dry press cloth over each piece and, supporting the weight of the iron at all times, allow steam from the iron to penetrate the fabric. Or, pin each section to shape, mist lightly with water, and allow to dry.

To block a project after joining, pin the item to the finished measurements, then block it following the procedures explained above.

CROCHETING INSTRUCTIONS

Working a Foundation Chain

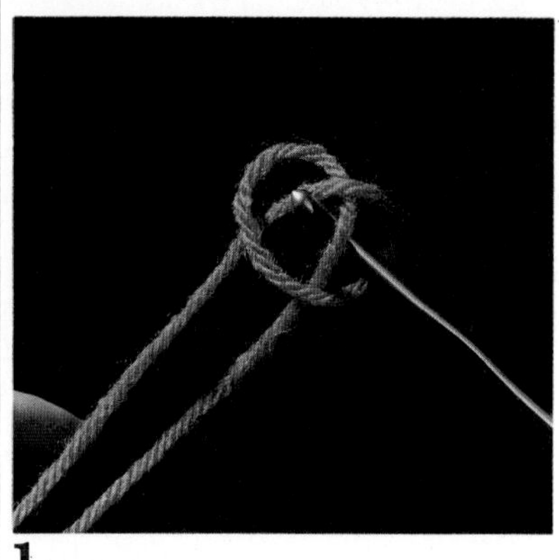

1

The slip knot: The slip knot is always the first loop on the hook. With the short end of the yarn lying across your left hand, loop yarn into a pretzel shape as shown in the photograph, *above.* Then insert the hook over the top of the outside strand on the right and *under* the next strand. Pull on both tails to tighten the loop on the hook.

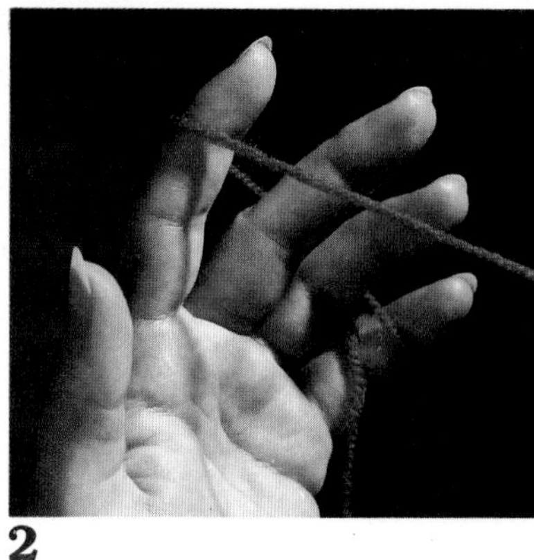

2

Holding the yarn in the left hand: Using the strand coming from the ball of yarn and your right hand (still holding the slip knot on the hook), wrap the yarn completely around the little finger of your left hand, and carry it across the back of the three middle fingers. Allow the yarn to slide across the tip of the index finger as you work.

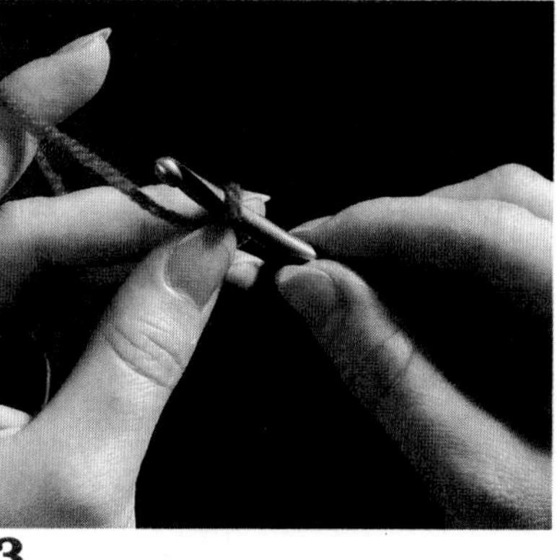

3

Holding the hook in the right hand: Hold the hook, with the slip knot on it, in your right hand as though you were holding a piece of chalk. With the tips of thumb and middle finger of the left hand, hold the knot below the slip knot as shown in photograph, *above.*

Single Crochet

1

Ch 20; * insert hook from front to back under top 2 loops of *second* chain (photo 1). Wrap yarn over hook; draw strand through the chain stitch only—2 loops are on the hook. Wrap yarn around hook (photo 2); draw strand through both loops on hook—1 sc made.

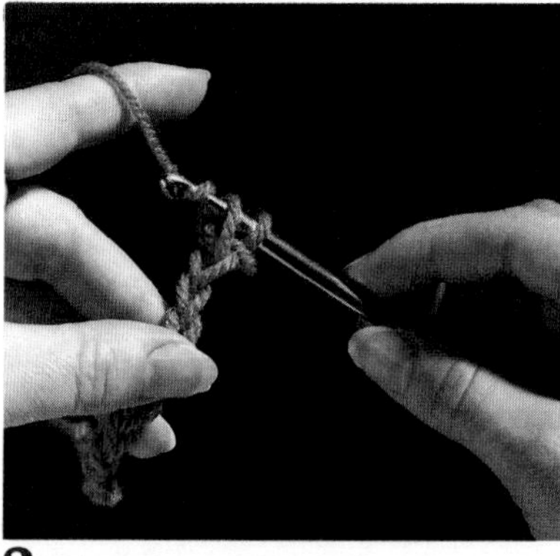

2

Working in *each* chain across the row (do not skip any chains), repeat from the * until all chains have been worked—19 single crochets. Then chain 1 and without removing the hook from the work, turn the work from right to left to begin working the next row.

3

Notice the chains running across the top of each single crochet on the first row of stitches. These chains are the top 2 loops you will work under on the next row. After you turned your work, these chains were not visible. However, when you insert the hook in the tiny

4

Making a chain: * With the hook lying across the front of the yarn strand leading to the index finger, wrap the yarn around the hook (yo) and pull the strand through the loop on the hook—1 chain made. Repeat from the * 19 times more. When working a foundation chain, the slip knot *never* counts as a chain stitch.

5

Working in the chains: Hold the strand of chains with the left hand, so the *flat* side of the chains face you. Three strands of yarn make up each chain. When working the first row of stitches in the length of chains, unless stated otherwise, always work under the two top strands (lps) of the chain (or any stitch) as shown in photo, *above*.

holes that appear below the top of the stitch, photo 3, you will be slipping your hook under the top 2 strands of the stitch.

To begin the second row, skip the chain-1 turning stitch and work a single crochet in the first single crochet as the work now faces you. Work a single crochet in each single crochet across the row—19 single crochet; then chain 1, turn. To make a practice swatch, continue to work a single crochet in each single crochet across the row and chain 1 at the end of each row before turning to begin a new row.

Crocheting Abbreviations

beg ....begin(ning)
bl ....block
CC ....contrasting color
ch ....chain
cl ....cluster
dc ....double crochet
dec ....decrease
dtr ....double treble crochet
grp ....group
hdc ....half-double crochet
inc ....increase
LH ....left hand
lp(s) ....loop(s)
MC ....main color
pat ....pattern
pc ....popcorn
rem ....remaining
RH ....right hand
rep ....repeat
rnd ....round
sc ....single crochet
sk ....skip
sl st ....slip stitch
sp ....space
st(s) ....stitch(es)
tog ....together
trc ....treble crochet
yo ....yarn over
* ....repeat from * as indicated
( )...repeat between ( )s as indicated
[ ]...repeat between [ ]s as indicated

Half-Double Crochet

1

Working on the same swatch as already established, complete a row of single crochets; then chain 2 and turn work. This chain-2 will now count as the first stitch of the row. * Referring to photo 1, wrap yarn over hook, and insert hook in the *second* single crochet of the row below (under 2 top loops).

2

Wrap yarn over hook (photo 2), and draw strand through the single crochet only—3 loops on hook. Wrap yarn over hook (photo 3), and draw strand through all 3 loops on hook—1 half-double crochet made. Working in *each* single crochet across the row (do not skip any stitches), repeat from the * across the row—18 half-double crochets made plus the turning chain-2 at the beginning of the row. Chain 2, and turn work.

3

To begin working the second row of half-double crochets, skip the first half-double crochet as the work now faces you, and repeat from the * across the row, working half-double crochets in the top of each half-double crochet; work the last half-double crochet in top of chain-2 at beginning of the previous row (work in the 2 top loops of the chain to avoid a hole in your work); then chain 2, turn.

Double Crochet

1

Working on the same swatch as already established, complete a row of half-double crochets, then chain 3 and turn work. This chain-3 will count as the first stitch of the next row. * Referring to photo 1, wrap yarn over hook, and insert hook in the *second* half-double crochet of the row below (under 2 top loops), wrap yarn over hook (photo 2), and draw strand through the half double crochet stitch only—3 loops on hook. Wrap yarn over hook (photo 3), and draw strand through just 2 loops on hook—2 loops on hook; wrap yarn over hook, and draw strand through 2 loops on hook (photo 4)—1 double crochet made. Working in *each* half double crochet across the row (do not skip any stitches), repeat from the * across the row—18 double crochets made plus the turning chain-3 at beginning of row; chain 3, and turn.

2

3

To begin working the second row of double crochets, skip the first double crochet as the work now faces you, and repeat from the * across the row, working a double crochet in top of each double crochet and work the last double crochet in top of the chain-3 at beginning of the previous row (work in the 2 top lps of the chain to avoid a hole in the work); then chain 3 and turn work.

Treble Crochet

1

Working on the same swatch as already established, complete a row of double crochets, then chain 4 and turn work. This chain-4 will count as the first stitch of the row. * Referring to photo 1, wrap yarn over hook 2 times, and insert hook in the second double crochet of the row below (under 2 top loops). Wrap yarn over hook (photo 2), and draw strand through the double crochet stitch only—4 loops on hook. Wrap yarn over hook (photo 3), and draw strand through 2 loops on hook—3 loops remain on hook; wrap yarn over hook and draw strand through 2 loops on hook—2 loops on hook; wrap yarn over hook and draw strand through last 2 loops on hook—1 treble crochet made.

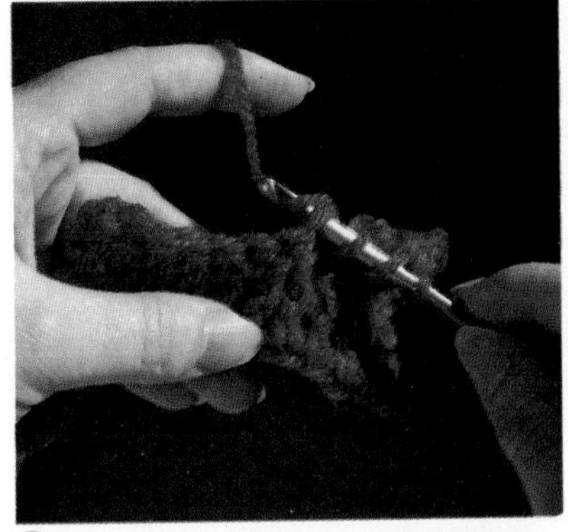

2

Working in each double crochet across the row, rep from the * across the row—18 treble crochets made plus the turning chain-4 at beginning of row; then chain 4 and turn work.

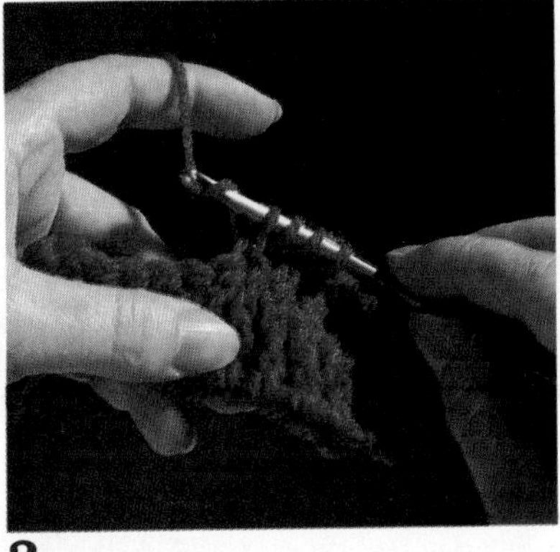

3

To begin working the second row of treble crochets, skip the first treble crochet as the work now faces you, and repeat from the * across the row, working a treble crochet in top of each treble crochet and work the last treble crochet in top of the chain-4 at beginning of the previous row; then chain 4 and turn work to begin the next row.

4

Continue to work double crochets in each double crochet across the row to work the practice swatch and work the chain 3 at end of each row before turning the work to begin a new row.

Slip Stitch

A slip stitch is used as a joining stitch when working in rounds, or to bind and strengthen edges. It is frequently used in knitting to finish neckline and sleeve edges.

Working on the swatch as already established, complete a row of treble crochet, then chain 1 and turn work. * Insert hook in the first treble crochet, wrap yarn over hook (photo 1), and draw strand through the treble crochet and the loop on the hook—1 slip stitch made. Working in each treble crochet, repeat from the * across the row.

Fasten off

At end of row, snip yarn, leaving a 6-inch tail. Wrap yarn over hook and draw the cut end through the loop on the hook. This last step knots the last stitch so the work will not unravel. Weave the cut strand into the back of the finished work. The words "end off" and "break off" are synonymous with "fasten off." All mean that you are finished working with the thread or yarn at this point in your work.

Stitching in the foundation chain

It is important to begin the first row of a pattern by working the first stitch in the appropriate chain. When starting a row of single crochet after completing the foundation chain, work the first single crochet in the *second* chain from the hook; work a half double crochet in the *third* chain, a double crochet in the *fourth* chain, and a treble crochet in the *fifth* chain. Except in rows of single crochet, the group of chains preceding the first stitch counts as the first stitch in the next row.

Keeping tension even

To keep stitches even and uniform in size, crochet over the *shank* of the hook. You will have better control over your stitching if you keep moving the thumb and middle finger of your left hand close to the area where you are stitching. To avoid stitching too tightly, draw up the loop in the stitch you are making and allow this loop to be almost twice as large as the loop already on the hook. As a result, when you complete each stitch, the work will be soft and flexible rather than stiff.

Working in rows

As you finish each row of stitching, you must turn your work over to begin the next row. Notice that you are working on the *wrong* side of the stitches of the previous row. Also, notice the tiny holes at the tops of the stitches. Insert the hook into these holes so each stitch in the row you are now going to work lies to the *left* of each stitch in the previous row. Keep this in mind as you work, especially when you work patterns that skip stitches.

At the end of each row you will work a "turning chain" to begin the next row. Turning chains raise the level of your work along the edge to equal the height of the stitches of the next row. Work the required number of chains, then without removing the hook, turn the work over to begin the next row.

With the exception of the single crochet, all turning chains count as the first stitch of the row. The following are guidelines for establishing the number of chains when working a straight-edged piece.

To begin a row of single crochet, chain 1, turn, and work the first single crochet in the first stitch of the row. For a row of half double crochet, chain 2, turn, and work the first half double in the second stitch of the row. To begin a row of double crochet, chain 3, turn, and work the first double crochet in the second stitch of the row. For a row of treble crochet, chain 4, turn, and work the first treble crochet in the second stitch of the row.

The last stitch of each row is worked in the top of the turning chain, except for the single crochet. Always work into two loops of the chain to avoid a hole in your work.

Working in rounds

Unlike patterns crocheted back and forth in rows, motifs such as circles, hexagons, some squares, and other medallion shapes are stitched in rounds that begin in the center. When you have stitched completely around the shape, you have completed one round. In most instances, you work with the right side facing you; the stitches are on the *right* side of the work. As you crochet each stitch, insert the hook into the hole to the *right* of the stitch in the round below (the opposite when working in rows).

Increases are a part of the pattern, and instructions cite specifically the stitches required to keep the work lying flat. As the motif increases in size, so will the number of stitches in each round.

Most rounds are joined by working a slip stitch into the top of the beginning chain. Work this slip stitch in two loops of the chain to avoid a hole in your work.

Working in the back loops

Working stitches in the *back* loops results in a ridge on the side that faces you. When directions are not specific, always work under the *two top loops* of the stitches. Pattern directions will indicate when to work in the *back* loops.

Working in the *back* loops means you work in the back single strand of the stitch of the previous row. When working in rounds, this strand lies along the rim of the outside edge; when working in rows, you must tilt your work to locate the strand.

Also, the pattern may indicate you are to work in the *front* loops of the stitches, creating a ridge on the opposite side. In this case, work the stitches in the *front* strand of the stitch below.

Working increases

Increasing makes your crochet piece wider or fuller. In most instances increasing is used for garment shaping or to achieve pattern effects. Increases can be worked any place in a row or round, although pattern instructions usually specify where and when they occur. The most common method of increasing is to work two stitches into one stitch in the previous row or round.

When instructions indicate increases are to be "evenly spaced" across the row or round, it is best to first calculate the number of stitches between each increase before beginning the next row or round. For example, when you are working on a piece that is 80 stitches and the directions tell you to increase 10 stitches evenly spaced, divide 10 into 80 to determine that on every eighth stitch you need to work an increase.

Working decreases

Decreasing makes your crochet piece narrower. Like increasing, it is used for garment shaping or pattern effects. The method of decreasing depends on the stitch you are using. Here are instructions for each stitch:

SINGLE CROCHET: Single crochet to the stitch preceding where the decrease begins, then draw up a loop in *each* of the next 2 single crochets. Wrap yarn over the hook and draw the strand through all 3 loops on the hook. One stitch is made from working over two.

HALF DOUBLE CROCHET: Work half double crochets to the stitch preceding where the decrease begins. Then wrap yarn over hook and draw up a loop in *each* of the next 2 half double crochets; wrap yarn over the hook and draw the strand through all 4 loops on the hook. One stitch is made from working over two.

DOUBLE CROCHET: Work double crochets to the stitch preceding where the decrease begins. Then wrap yarn over the hook and draw up a loop in the next double crochet; wrap yarn over the hook and draw strand through 2 loops on the hook. Wrap yarn over the hook and draw up a loop in the *next* double crochet; wrap yarn over the hook and draw through 2 loops on hook; then wrap yarn over hook and draw through remaining 3 loops on hook. One stitch is made from working over two.

TREBLE CROCHET: Work treble crochets to the stitch preceding where the decrease begins. Then wrap the yarn over the hook twice and draw up a loop in the next treble crochet; (wrap yarn over the hook and draw the strand through 2 loops on the hook) twice. Wrap the yarn around the hook twice and draw up a loop in the *next* treble crochet; (wrap yarn over the hook and draw strand through 2 loops on the hook) twice; wrap yarn around the hook, and draw through the remaining 3 loops on the hook. One stitch is made from working over two.

Errors in your work

Correcting mistakes in crocheted work is easy. Simply remove the hook from the work and pull out the stitches until the error is removed. Establish where you are in your pattern and continue crocheting from that point.

Left-handed crocheters

If you are left-handed and unable to find someone to teach you to crochet, you might want to learn to stitch right-handed. Keep in mind that even beginning right-hand crocheters have a difficult time learning to hold the hook and thread. The left hand is just as important as the right hand and the two must work together to produce even and uniform stitches. By all means, continue to practice. Once you succeed in learning to stitch, it will be much simpler for you to obtain help when problems arise.

Uses of basic crochet stitches

Once you have mastered the basic crochet stitches, you easily can create many different pattern stitches. For example, you can use them in combination to form shells, popcorns, clusters, picots, and many lacy patterns. The information and tips below will help you follow pattern directions:

Many instructions call for working several stitches in a single stitch of the previous row. Read the instructions carefully, paying special attention to these stitches and where they are worked. For example, the pattern may read "work 5 dc *in the next sc*" *or* "work sc, hdc, dc, hdc, sc *in the next sc*." This means that in one stitch you work all the above stitches.

In addition to working in the stitches of the row below, you may work in spaces or loops formed by chains in the row below. For example, the pattern may read, "in the next *ch-2 sp* work 3 dc, ch 2, 3 dc." This means that in the space (not in the chains), created by working a ch-2 in the row below, you will work 3 dc, ch 2, and 3 dc.

Sometimes you will need to work a stitch in the same row where you are working and not in the previous row. For example, the pattern may read, "dc in next dc, ch 3, *sl st in last dc made,* dc in next dc." This means after you complete the ch-3, you work a sl st in the dc you completed before the ch-3.

Filet crochet is a combination of open spaces (mesh) and blocks to create lovely lacy designs. Most patterns are worked with double crochet stitches and accompanied by a chart showing placement of blocks and spaces. A solid block on a chart represents 4 double crochet stitches; the open spaces are chain-2 loops.

When the next row begins with a block, chain 3 at the end of a row, both to turn and to count as the first stitch of the block of the next row. When the next row begins with a space, chain 5 at the end of a row to turn and to count as the first double crochet and the first chain 2 space.

Crochet a block over a space simply by working 2 double crochets in the chain-2 space in the row below. Crochet a space by working a chain-2 and skipping 2 double crochets in the row below.

For raised textured items, such as Irish crochet, instructions indicate stitches are worked around the post of a stitch in the row below from either the *front* or the *back*.

Work the stitch as you normally would, except do not work into the stitch (hole); instead, work around the upright bar created by the stitch.

When working around the stitch (post) from the *front,* insert the hook from the front, go around the back of the stitch, back to the front side of the appropriate stitch, and complete the stitch. When working around the stitch from the *back,* insert the hook from the back, go around the front of the stitch, return to the back of the appropriate stitch, and complete the stitch. The stitch behind the raised stitch is left unworked as you proceed across the row.

Casting on with 2 strands of yarn

1

Slip knot: The slip knot always is the first loop on the right-hand needle and counts as the first stitch on the row. With the short end of the yarn lying across the left hand, make the pretzel-shape loop shown *above.* Then insert the needle over the top of the outside strand on the right and *under* the next strand. Pull on both tails to tighten the loop on the needle.

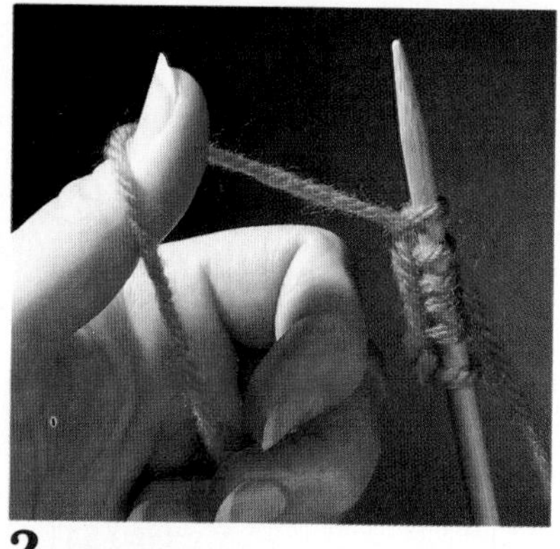

2

Holding the yarn in the left hand: Allowing approximately 1 inch of yarn for each stitch to be cast on, make a slip knot 20 inches from the end of the yarn to cast on 20 stitches. Referring to photo 2, *above,* wrap the *short* end around the left thumb and hold the remaining tail in place with the three back fingers of the left palm.

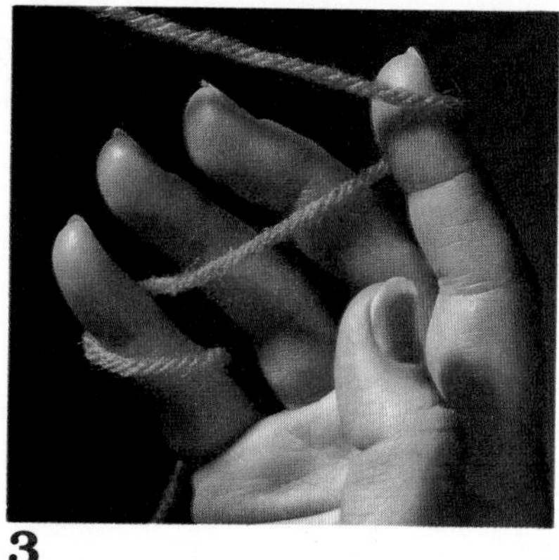

3

Temporarily holding the needle with the slip knot in the left hand, wrap the yarn coming from the ball in the right hand as shown in photo 3, *above.* Then return the needle to the right hand.

Working knit stitches

1

Begin to work with two needles, holding the needle with the cast-on stitches in the left hand. * With the yarn behind the work, insert the right needle *from the front* through the center of the first stitch on the left needle as shown on the photo, *above.*

2

Wrap the yarn in the right hand around the back and across the front of the right needle.

3

Slide the right-hand needle toward yourself, and at the same time, tilt the needle and draw the wrapped strand through the loop on the left-hand needle as shown in the photo, *above.*

4

* With the yarn behind the needle, drop the needle in the right hand toward the palm of the left hand. Referring to photo 4, *above,* insert the tip of the needle from front to back through the loop formed by the strand that is wrapped around the thumb.

5

Referring to photo, *above,* wrap the yarn in the right hand around the needle.

6

Slip the thumb loop over the needle as shown in photo, *above,* and let it slide from the thumb. Draw up the loop to fit the needle.

Repeat from * 18 times more—20 stitches on the needle.

4

With the index finger of the left hand, slip the first loop off the left needle (see photo, *above*), and drop from needle—1 knit stitch made. Repeat from the * in each of the stitches across the row. Then transfer the right-hand needle to the left hand and begin a new row.

Knitting Abbreviations

beg	begin(ning)
CC	contrasting color
dec	decrease
dp	double-pointed
inc	increase
k	knit
LH	left hand
lp(s)	loop(s)
MC	main color
p	purl
pat	pattern
psso	pass slip st over
rem	remaining
RH	right hand
rep	repeat
rnd	round
sc	single crochet
sk	skip
sl st	slip stitch
sp	space
st(s)	stitch(es)
st st	stockinette stitch
tbl	through back loop
tog	together
yo	yarn over
*	repeat from * as indicated
( )	repeat between ( )s as indicated
[ ]	repeat between [ ]s as indicated

Working purl stitches

1

Hold the needle with the stitches in the left hand. * With the yarn in *front* of the work, and referring to photo, *above,* insert the right needle *from the back* through the center of the first loop on the hook.

2

Wrap the yarn in the right hand around the back and across the front of the right needle as shown in the photo, *above.*

Slide the right needle toward you, and at the same time, catch the wrapped strand and "push" the strand through the loop on the left needle.

3

With the index finger of the left hand, slip the first loop from the left needle and drop it from the needle—1 purl stitch made.

Repeat from the * in each of the stitches across the row. Then transfer the right-hand needle to the left hand and begin a new row.

Binding off stitches

When you have completed the number of rows required in your knitting, you need to "bind off" these stitches to remove them from the needles.

Knit (or purl) the first two stitches. Then, referring to the photo, *above,* insert the tip of the left needle into the first stitch on the right needle and lift over the second stitch and drop from the needle—1 stitch has been bound off.

* Knit (or purl) the next stitch on the left needle, then lift the first stitch over the second stitch and drop it from the needle. Repeat from the * across the row until 1 stitch remains on the right needle. Cut yarn, leaving a 6-inch tail, and pull up loop with right needle until yarn passes through center of last stitch. To avoid a lumpy knot, do not pull the end of yarn through the last loop on the needle.

When you are working on a knit side, bind off stitches as if to knit; when working on a purl side, bind off stitches as if to purl. When binding off ribbing stitches, knit the knit stitches, and purl the purl stitches.

Increasing stitches

When you add more stitches to your knitting, the piece becomes wider. Increases are used to shape the work or to create patterns and textures.

There are many ways to work increases in your work, and they all will influence the appearance of your knitting. The three most common ways to increase, and their effects on your knitting, follow.

KNITTING OR PURLING INTO THE SAME STITCH TWICE: This type of increasing is most frequently used, but it produces a small ridge on the surface of the knitted fabric when you are working in stockinette stitch. It is best to use this method of increasing on the edges of your work.

When working an increase by *knitting* into the same stitch twice, knit the stitch as usual from the front of the stitch, but *do not drop* the stitch from the left-hand needle. Increase by inserting the tip of the right-hand needle into the *back* loop of the same stitch (from front to back). Wrap the yarn around the right-hand needle and draw the yarn through the back of the stitch. Then drop the stitch from the left-hand needle.

To work an increase by *purling* into the same stitch twice, purl the stitch as usual, but *do not remove* the stitch from the left-hand needle. Take the tip of the right-hand needle around to the *back* of the left needle, insert the tip into the *left side* of the back loop, and bring it to the front of the work. Wrap the yarn around the right needle as for a regular purl stitch and complete the stitch. Then drop the stitch from the left needle.

YARN-OVER INCREASES: Yarn-over increases often are found on raglan sleeve shapings, lacy patterns, and beadings on booties and other edges to run cord or ribbons through. Work them as follows:

To increase between two *knit stitches* bring the yarn to the front of the work (as if to purl) and wrap it (yo) *counterclockwise* around the front of the right needle and return to the back of the work. Then knit the next stitch on the left-hand needle. This method produces a small hole below the stitch.

To increase between two *purl stitches,* take the yarn completely around the right needle (yo) *counterclockwise,* and return to the front. Then purl the next stitch.

INCREASING IN THE RUNNING STRAND: This method of increasing is the least noticeable when working garments and the most suitable for stockinete stitch.

When using this method on the *knit* side of your work, work up to the point where the increase is to be made. Insert the tip of the right needle, from the back, into the running loop before the next stitch and place the loop on the left needle. Then knit into the *back* of this loop.

On the purl side of your work, work up to the point where the increase is made. Insert the tip of the right needle, from the front, into the running strand before the next stitch and place the loop on the left needle. Then purl the loop as you normally would.

In both of these methods, the finished stitch will appear twisted. This twist is necessary to avoid a hole in the succeeding row.

Decreasing stitches

Your knitting piece becomes narrower when you decrease. Like increases, decreases are used to shape knitted fabric and create patterns. The most common methods of decreases follow.

WORKING TWO STITCHES TOGETHER: The simplest way to work a decrease is to knit or purl 2 stitches together. When decreasing *knitwise,* the resulting stitch slants to the right. Insert the tip of the right needle into the front of the *second* stitch, then into the first stitch on the left needle. Wrap the yarn around the right needle and draw the strand through both stitches on the left needle and complete the stitch.

When decreasing *purlwise,* insert the tip of the right needle through the first stitch, then through the second stitch on the left needle, wrap yarn around the right needle and draw strand through both stitches to complete the stitch.

PASS THE SLIP STITCH OVER: A method of decreasing similar to binding off is to slip 1, knit 1, and pass the slipped stitch over the knit stitch. This decrease is written *sl 1, k 1, psso* or *skp.* Work up to the point for the decrease, then insert the right needle into the next stitch on the left needle as if to knit and slip it to the right-hand needle (do not knit it). Knit the next stitch. With tip of left needle, lift the slipped stitch over the knit stitch and drop from needle.

This method of decreasing is almost always worked on the *knit* side of the work. The resulting stitch slants to the left.

To slip a stitch

A slip stitch is made simply by transferring a stitch from one needle to another without working it. Insert the right needle into the stitch on the left needle from the back, as if to purl. Then slip the stitch onto the right needle without working or twisting it. Always slip a stitch *purlwise* unless directions specify otherwise or when working the sl 1, k 1, psso decrease.

When working on the *knit* side, do *not* bring the yarn forward to slip the stitch *unless* the instructions indicate the yarn is to be brought forward before slipping the stitch.

When working on the *purl* side, keep the yarn at the front when slipping the next stitch (do not take the yarn to the back of the work).

Changing needles

Instructions frequently require that you change needles from one size to another on the same piece of knitting. For example, when working a sweater, the ribbing portions at hip, neckline, and sleeves may be worked with a smaller-size needle than the remaining portions of the sweater. Two rows of knitting are required to change needles from one size to another.

Work the piece of knitting to the point where you change needle size. Then put aside the free needle and begin the next row with the new size needle. At the end of that row, drop the free needle and work the following row with the second new needle.

ACKNOWLEDGMENTS

We wish to express our appreciation to the designers, photographers, and others who contributed to this book. When more than one project appears on a page, the acknowledgment specifically cites the page number. A page number alone indicates one designer or source contributed all of the project material listed for that page.

Our special thanks to the following designers, who contributed projects to this book.

Gary Boling—12, crocheted scarf; 13, checked scarf; 42–43; 64
Judith Brandeau—136–137, collar
Joan Cravens—108–109
Laura Holtorf Collins—130–131
Katherine Davidson for Tahki Yarns—68–69
Jackie Davis and Mary Stoy—52–53
Susan Douglas—22–23; 129, knitted kitten toys
Dixie Falls—12–13, all hats and mittens; 24; 36–37; 38–39, 61; 106–107; 117, sachets
Eloise Kellam—134–135
Gail Kinkead—90; 108–109, curtains; 116
Knit Wits of Iowa—138
Estella Lacy—165
Bonnie Schermerhorn—11; 139
Linda Sparkman—63
Sara Jane Treinen—8–9; 25; 62; 104–105; 110–111; 114–115; 128–129, blanket; 132–133; 155, hat; 162–163
Jim Williams—160–161
Dee Wittmack—54–55

We also are pleased to acknowledge the following photographers, whose talents and technical skills contributed much to this book.

Ross Chapple—58-59
Mike Dieter—37, detail; 54–55; 56–57; 61; 88, detail; 104–105; 106–107; 108–109; 111, detail; 112; 114–115; 128–129; 131; 132–133; 134–135; 154–155; 156–157; 158–159; 164; 166, detail; 185
Hedrich-Blessing—10–11
Thomas Hooper—25; 26–27; 38–39; 40–41; 60; 64–65; 66–67; 68–69; 158, detail; 160–161; 180–181; 182–183;
Hopkins Associates—52–53; 63; 117; 166–167
Scott Little—7, detail; 8–9; 22–23; 24; 36-37; 42–43; 66, detail; 88-89; 110–111; 113; 116; 130; 136–137; 162–163; 165;
Bradley Olman—6–7; 184, top; 186–187;
Perry Struse—12–13; 62; 7; 90–91; 92–93; 138–139; 184, bottom;

For their cooperation and courtesy, we extend a special thanks to the following sources for designs and projects.

Anny Blatt—180–181
24770 Crestview
Farmington Hills, MI 48018

The Bucilla Company—6–7; 187
150 Meadowlands Parkway
P.O. Box 1534
Secaucus, NJ 07094

Coats & Clark Inc.—26–27; 40–41; 65; 92–93; 113, napkin; 117, edging; 182–183; 184, gloves; 186
72 Cummings Point Road
Stamford, CT 06902

Crystal Palace Yarns—66, vest
3006 San Pablo Avenue
Berkeley, CA 94702

Lacis, Antique Lace & Textiles
112–113, crocheted flowers
2990 Adeline Street
Berkeley, CA 94703

Lily Craft Products—154–155, place mat
B. Blumenthal and Co., Inc.
140 Kero Road
Carlstadt, NJ 07072

Lion Brand Yarn Co.—58–59
1270 Broadway
New York, NY 10001

Caroline Moon—13

Phildar—60; 117, baskets
6438 Dawson Boulevard
Norcross, GA 30093

Pingouin Corp.—10
P.O. Box 100
Highway 45
Jamestown, SC 29453

Soft Antiques—166, pillow
43 Main Street
Box 1826
Orleans, MA 02653

Talon-American Thread—88–89
High Ridge Park
Stamford, CT 06905

William Unger and Company, Inc.
—67, cardigan
230 Fifth Avenue
New York, NY 10001

We would like to thank the following sources, who provided support in developing material for this book.

Brunswick Yarns
P.O. Box 548
Moosup, CT 06354

DMC
107 Trumbull St
Elizabeth, NJ 07206

Paternayan Yarns
Johnson Creative Arts
445 Main Street
West Townsend, MA 01474

Tahki Imports Ltd.
82 Kennedy Street
Hackensack, NJ 07601

William Unger and Company, Inc.
230 Fifth Avenue
New York, NY 10001

INDEX

For photographs, see pages noted in **bold** type; remaining numbers refer to instruction pages.